TAURUS
21 APRIL – 21 MAY

First published in Great Britain 2013
by Mills & Boon, an imprint of Harlequin (UK) Limited,
Eton House, 18-24 Paradise Road, Richmond, Surrey TW9 1SR

HOROSCOPES 2014 © Dadhichi Toth 2013

ISBN: 978 0 263 91095 7

Cover design by Anna Viniero
Typeset by Midland Typesetters

Harlequin (UK) policy is to use papers that are natural, renewable and recyclable products and made from wood grown in sustainable forests. The logging and manufacturing processes conform to the legal environmental regulations of the country of origin.

Printed and bound in Spain
by Blackprint CPI, Barcelona

Dedicated to

The Light of Intuition

Sri V. Krishnaswamy—mentor and friend

Special thanks to

Nyle Cruz for her tireless support and suggestions

Thanks to

Joram and Isaac for hanging in there

Additional appreciation to

Devika Adlakha for her excellent editorial support

ABOUT DADHICHI

Dadhichi is one of Australia's foremost astrologers and is frequently seen on television and in other media. He has the unique ability to draw from complex astrological theory to provide clear, easily understandable advice and insights for people who want to know what their futures may hold.

In the 29 years that Dadhichi has been practising astrology, face reading and other esoteric studies, he has conducted over 10,000 consultations. His clients include celebrities, political and diplomatic figures, and media and corporate identities from all over the world.

Dadhichi's unique blend of astrology and face reading helps people fulfill their true potential. His extensive experience practising Western astrology is complemented by his research into the theory and practice of Eastern forms of astrology.

Dadhichi has been a guest on many Australian television shows, and several of his political and worldwide forecasts have proved uncannily accurate. He appears regularly on Australian television networks and is a columnist for online and offline Australian publications.

His websites—www.astrology.com.au and www.facereader.com— attract hundreds of thousands of visitors each month and offer a wide variety of features, helpful information and services.

MESSAGE FROM DADHICHI

Hello once again and welcome to your 2014 horoscope!

Time and Speed are the governors of our lives these days. There's *never enough* time, and the hectic pace at which we move is getting *too much* to handle. So we oscillate between never enough and too much. We are either too slow in finishing our tasks, or the hands of the clock appear to be whizzing forward, especially when we're under pressure. We are constantly trying to create more time just to keep up with everyone else. And all those people are rushing out of control. What is this madness? We need to reclaim control of our lives and bring these terrible twins of speed and time under our control if we are ever to master our destinies.

According to Einstein and his incredible theory of relativity, speed and time are related. The faster we move, the quicker time flies. As we crank up the pace of our lives, time is impacted upon even more. You don't need me to tell you that; your experience will remind you of this fact every day, especially when you look in the mirror and see an additional wrinkle or two from time to time. Age is the favourite child of these two parents: speed and time. In the old days, it used to be the elderly who complained about the pace of time. But now, everyone, even youngsters, grumble about how little time they have and how they are forever trying to cram as much fun and experience into the moment. This attitude seems to be the order of the day, yet it will never, ever be enough.

The planets also operate on the same principle of speed and time, and this is how we generate astrological forecasts. Speed is related to the distance these planets traverse around the Sun, and the time it takes for them to do their celestial dance around the Sun is referred to as a planetary cycle.

We often talk about being in harmony with our environment and leaving as invisible a carbon footprint as we can, thus re-establishing natural equilibrium on earth. But our larger celestial environment is something we've overlooked. Ancient astrologers, however, knew the secret of our interconnectedness to the greater environment, and they gave us esoteric spiritual techniques for tuning in to these controllers of our fate. But how do you control the planets, let alone speed and time? It is through intuition, perception and self-awareness. By developing your perception and intuitive faculties, you will be one of the survivors in this brave new world.

If you're up to the challenge, this will increase your psychic abilities, thereby helping you surmount the obstacles of speed and time. You will bring yourself into harmony with your own physical, mental and emotional needs, and you will be able to tune easily in to your environment and fellow man. You will sense what these planetary energies are doing to you and can adjust yourself accordingly. This requires the subtle art of spiritual listening. This is not the hearing that is done with your ears. This is listening done with the heart. Through these simple techniques you *will* conquer time!

Our frames of reference are changing, and our ability to adapt to the light-speed pace is demanding refinements and adjustments in perception. In 2014, take the time to move at your own pace and look at what it is *you* want to achieve, not what is foisted upon you by culture, family and the establishment. Run your own race, and even if you are moving in high gear, at least you will be the one in control, not the clock. Use the transits and forecasts in the last chapter to help you gain an overview of the likely time of events. By taking control of your time and slowing the pace of life, you begin to control your destiny. In doing so, you rediscover the pleasure of your own self and the talents that you have been endowed with. This will then be a time of self-empowerment and great fulfilment.

Your astrologer,

Dadhichi Toth

CONTENTS

CONTENTS
CONTINUED

CONTENTS
CONTINUED

TAURUS
PROFILE

YOU'VE GOTTA DANCE LIKE THERE'S
NOBODY WATCHING, LOVE LIKE YOU'LL
NEVER BE HURT, SING LIKE THERE'S
NOBODY LISTENING, AND LIVE LIKE
IT'S HEAVEN ON EARTH.

William W. Purkey

TAURUS SNAPSHOT

Key Life Phrase		I Possess
Zodiac Totem		The Bull
Zodiac Symbol		
Zodiac Facts		Second sign of the zodiac; fixed, fruitful, feminine and moist
Zodiac Element		Earth
Key Characteristics		Unyielding, sensual, steadfast, devoted, self-assured, self-righteous, headstrong, security-conscious and decisive
Compatible Star Signs		Virgo, Gemini, Cancer, Capricorn, Pisces and Aries

Mismatched Signs		Leo, Libra, Scorpio, Sagittarius and Aquarius
Ruling Planet		Venus
Love Planets		Mercury and Mars
Finance Planet		Mercury
Speculation Planet		Mercury
Career Planets		Saturn and Uranus
Spiritual and Karmic Planets		Saturn
Friendship Planets		Neptune and Jupiter
Destiny Planet		Mercury
Famous Taureans		Al Pacino, Penélope Cruz, Shirley MacLaine, Cate Blanchett, Renée Zellweger, Saddam Hussein, Kirsten Dunst, James Brown, George Clooney, Janet Jackson, Carmen Electra, David Beckham, Yehudi Menuin, Jack Nicholson, Barbra Streisand, Carol Burnett, Uma Thurman, Joe Lewis, Cher and Andy MacDowell
Lucky Numbers and Significant Years		5, 6, 8, 14, 15, 17, 23, 24, 26, 32, 33, 35, 41, 42, 44, 50, 51, 53, 59, 60, 62, 68, 69, 77, 80

Lucky Gems	Diamond, quartz crystal, aquamarine, lapis lazuli and emerald
Lucky Fragrances	Sandalwood, jasmine and rose
Affirmation/Mantra	I am secure and without need.
Lucky Days	Wednesday, Friday and Saturday

TAURUS OVERVIEW

Honesty personified, you call a spade is a spade, whether others like it or not. You are enormously inclined towards commitments and genuine in friendships. At the same time, you have a tendency to withdraw into your reserved and introverted self. It is at such moments that you should voice your thoughts, regardless of external disagreement.

Your personality powerfully radiates fortitude, persistence and fidelity, which are defining traits for you, Taurus. However, not everyone agrees with your thoughts and style of living, as you have an exacting way of getting things done. This may bring negativity, but that's the least of your concerns. Having made up your mind, you remain unmoved, and even seemingly sane advice cannot compel you to alter your decisions.

You take immense pleasure in soaking yourself in material wealth. It's no wonder; the comfort of good living and luxury has always fascinated you. This overindulgence may sometimes have serious repercussions on your health and wellbeing, so moderate food cravings, alcohol intake and excesses of any kind—even in bed!

PRAGMATIC TAURUS

As an earth sign, you are intrinsically secure and pragmatic. You are the last person to aid another in building castles in the air. Instead of an unreliable venture, you prefer the tried and tested with a known outcome.

You're driven by a fierce need for security. But this is not because you're self-obsessed! The fear of destitution and dependence on others constantly lurks in your being. This persistent thought governs your actions and happens to be the key reason for your hardworking spirit. You work to secure your family's future, but you get so overwhelmed by your sense of responsibility that it robs you of the pleasure of enjoying life. Before you know it, this beautiful gift passes right before your eyes because you are too focused on a future that is yet to come!

You are clearly not adept at dealing with situations where others call the shots. If you are in a submissive role, you may bow to authority and follow the herd, but don't expect this to last long. Your Bull's nature will eventually reveal itself and you will seize command of your own finances and destiny. At the same time, your indolence may land you in grave circumstances, creating utter disharmony. You are happiest with a set of goals that allow you to be in absolute control of your own destiny.

You're ambitious, but your style is never cut-throat. Rushing to cross the finish line is not your definition of ambition. The old adage 'slow and steady wins the race' perfectly outlines your attitude towards life. You may not be a top-speed achiever, but you realise your goals in a manner that allows other aspects of your life to flourish. By and large, Taurus individuals are not opportunists or gamblers.

You are not someone who allows others to toss you around and treat you shoddily. You work at a steady pace and on your own terms to ensure things are done in the correct fashion. You detest working towards goals in a scattered manner. Your idea of perfection is striving for quality in the work that you do.

You exude two beautiful qualities: tolerance and compassion. You're not caught up in the intellectual complexities of life, so you possess an uncanny knack of helping others with their problems. You can be unbelievably impartial, even in the face of contradictory viewpoints, which is another endearing quality. Perseverance, a non-judgmental ear and an innately caring self are just some of the personality traits that make Taurus so special.

TAURUS CUSPS

ARE YOU A CUSP BABY?

Being born on the crossover of two star signs means you have the qualities of both. Sometimes you don't know whether you're Arthur or Martha! Some of my clients can't quite figure out whether they are indeed their own star sign or the one before or after. This is to be expected because being born on the borderline means you take on both qualities. The following will give you an overview of the subtle effects of these cusp dates and how they affect your personality quite significantly.

Taurus–Aries Cusp

You are fiercely independent, especially with the additional character traits of Aries. If you were born between the 21st and the 28th of April, you are bound to exhibit traits of the Ram.

Along with the fiery aspects of Aries, you are reliable, hugely devoted and somewhat inflexible. You are exceptionally adept at articulating your creative pursuits with immense vigour and persuasion. Since you have an enormous desire to realise your ambitions, you can also be ruthless, thanks to your Taurean Bull instincts. In fact, you are forever in a combative and volatile mode lest someone challenge you or cross your path.

Since Aries-born individuals are outrageously outspoken, you will unhesitatingly speak your mind, even at the cost of sounding unpleasant. The influence of Mars also gives you a volcanic surge of energy, which can make your demands on others too impractical and strenuous to cope with.

> ### *Financial Security*
>
> You are blessed with monetary comfort as you strive for financial success and independence. Even if don't enjoy plentiful material wealth in the early stages of your life, you will steadily work towards securing it.

Abstain from locking horns with others and practise flexibility instead, a quality you stand to benefit from. You are likely to focus solely on yourself, and this lack of sensitivity to others may spell catastrophe for your relationships. Listen and extend humility towards others. These factors are necessary for building a harmonious social and marital relationship.

Taurus–Gemini Cusp

Gemini lends a fascinating intellectual twist to your typically tenacious and indomitable Taurus self. If you were born in the last week of Taurus, between the 15th and the 21st of May, you will exhibit a mixture of influences from your Sun sign of Taurus and Gemini.

The typical Venus influence on your Taurus Sun sign is accelerated by the Mercurial and Gemini influence. Unlike the characteristic Gemini, who struggles with stabilising thought, you translate your imagination and curiosity in a practical way. You have the ability to articulate your thoughts with greater clarity and steadiness, and you use these qualities creatively to achieve greater success in life.

Although you embody the vigour and resolve of your Taurus Sun sign, you're also influenced by Gemini's intellectual and inquisitive tendencies. You communicate thoughtfully and are never inclined to pursue any unrealistic ideas. Rather, you delve in fascinating endeavours that enhance your life and lend much-desired security for your family and loved ones.

You're never in danger of being too impulsive or precariously outspoken, as you possess the ability to put yourself in another person's shoes and know exactly how they will react. This ability to empathise and offer practical and genuine advice wins the trust of many seeking assistance from you. You're also a glib conversationalist who makes a lasting impression on others and believes in sharing their experiences to benefit the community and world at large.

Some people may judge you for your fickle-mindedness, but the truth is that you're not indecisive; you just like to measure all alternatives before taking the plunge. You carefully weigh your options to ensure an exceptional outcome and to avoid hidden snags. It's only after this thorough homework that you commit yourself to the task at hand.

You are likely to be highly opinionated, with a complete disregard for other people's point of view. You like to prove a point and rob others of the opportunity to express themselves. Try not to be too focused on who's right or wrong; what matters most is the value you create out of it.

TAURUS CELEBRITIES

FAMOUS MALE:
GEORGE CLOONEY

George Clooney is synonymous with stunning good looks, a debonair manner and a charming personality—all which make up the so-called typical Taurus-born male. There is no denying that George has a unique quality that most of us can't resist. This is true star quality.

Venus endows a Taurus man with the ability to attract women, but it also creates difficulties with committing to a long-term relationship. George openly admits this. How often have we seen him with a new partner at an Emmy or Academy Awards event? The Taurus-born man loves variety and often has an insatiable attraction to sense experiences. These are not limited to sexual escapades. They include food, drink and other expensive and sometimes excessive tastes.

George likes to distinguish himself from other so-called playboys. When he was invited to a Playboy Mansion pyjama party, he said: 'I was hanging out with Leonardo DiCaprio and Jim Carrey. We were all sort of protecting one another; you don't want to seem like you're desperate.

I grew up with the magazine, so naturally I wanted to see the Grotto. When I got there, I was cornered by about 15 people, most of them pretty girls. But it's not like you might imagine. Instead, they all wanted to have their picture taken with me. When that happens, it's like you're a cardboard cut-out for people to stand next to.'

The Taurus man knows how to make money, and after his debut in *ER* (1994–1999), he was able to clinch some very big movie roles. Some of these include *Batman and Robin* (1997), *The Peacemaker* (1997), *Out of Sight* (1998), *Three Kings* (1999), *O Brother, Where Art Thou?* (2000), *The Perfect Storm* (2000), *Ocean's Eleven* (2001), *Syriana* (2005) and *Ocean's Thirteen* (2007). There is no doubt that George Clooney's need for Taurean security has been more than fulfilled!

FAMOUS FEMALE:
MEGAN FOX

Venus, named after the mythological goddess of beauty, is the ruling planet for Taurus. Megan Fox exemplifies this concept of beauty and sensuality, and it makes perfect sense that she was born under the second Zodiac sign of Taurus.

Many born under this sign are drawn to the arts, and acting in particular, so it comes as no surprise that Megan has become very successful in this field. There is also no doubt that she is a goddess to millions of adulating fans worldwide!

Women born under the sign of Taurus make wonderful mothers and homemakers, and sometimes we forget that even stars like Megan have this maternal instinct. She once said: 'No one believes me when I talk about this, but I'm really maternal. I worry that because I've always wanted [kids] so much ... I won't be able to have them, even though I would be able to provide them with such an amazing environment.' Individuals ruled by the sign of the Bull have a nurturing temperament, so having children would suit Megan perfectly. Megan gave birth to a son in 2012.

As much as they love family life and children, Taurus-born natives are also interested in material security, which is why they are usually financially successful at whatever they do. Megan started acting and modelling at the tender age of 13, and was fortunate enough to win awards at the 1999 American modelling and talent convention in South Carolina. Her film debut was in *Holiday in the Sun* (2001), but she catapulted to fame in *Transformers* (2007) and *Transformers: Revenge of the Fallen* (2009). Being a Taurus also means tenacity and determination, which are key aspects of her continuing success. There is no doubt that Megan will continue to achieve greater heights in her career as time goes by.

TAURUS

AT LARGE

A MAN SHOULD FIRST DIRECT HIMSELF
IN THE WAY HE SHOULD GO. ONLY THEN
SHOULD HE INSTRUCT OTHERS.

Buddha

TAURUS MAN

TAURUS MAN: SNAPSHOT

Ingenious

Robust

Unbending

Thorough

Finishes what he starts

Great provider

Sturdy and robust, Taurus men are usually big-boned with prominent necks and jaws. They also have a strong tendency to put on weight because of their unrestrained lifestyle.

Your personality, Taurus, is the absolute opposite of the fast-paced world around you. Your time management dates to a bygone era when life was more sluggish. You think time is always on your side and approach relationships, work and day-to-day activities with this blissful unhurriedness. You believe that haste makes waste.

Even though you are intensely opinionated, voicing your thoughts to people you are not comfortable with may be challenging. When you do choose to speak, your approach is far from conventional. You manifest an utterly dogmatic streak when stifled, especially on matters that challenge the beliefs you hold dear.

Many Taurean men strive for success at work and regard their responsibilities as priorities. This may be impressive, but not from the employer's point of view. The reason you get flak is because you are so precise in performing a job that you give no thought to the amount of time it is taking up. What matters to you is a job well done, and in your devotedness to this ideal, you become blissfully oblivious to deadlines.

While many may regard you as unsympathetic, coarse and insensible, you can also be the exact opposite. You are big-hearted, benevolent and gentle in your relationships with your family and friends. Your nurturing and protective instincts make you an unbelievably generous provider. It goes without saying that your idea of a fulfilling life is raising a happy family.

Clear communication is pivotal for the harmony you seek in personal relationships. With your know-it-all attitude, you run the risk of overlooking your partner's needs and creating differences instead. For the overall health of the relationship, it's crucial to take your partner into your confidence. Open-hearted dialogues that allow others to express their sentiments won't be easy with your deep-seated stubbornness. However, overcoming this tendency can help you go a long way in polishing your nature and adapting harmoniously to the environment.

Creative Taurus

Everyone knows that creativity runs in your veins. Hailing from the zodiac element of earth, your imaginative expressions are mostly practical in nature. Architecture, landscape design and other hands-on projects offer perfect avenues for your inventive Taurean abilities.

Speaking of the element of earth, I have met a multitude of Taurean men with an intrinsic passion for gardening. Many like to get their hands dirty and fondly watch over their lovely garden as it blooms in bounty. It gives them a wonderful feeling of tranquility, contentment and joy.

It is intriguing to note that the Zodiac sign pertaining to your evolution is the progressive sign of Aquarius. This means that your greatest challenge is surpassing your own limitations and excelling beyond the confines you draw for yourself. Seize the moment and live your life to the fullest.

✤ TAURUS WOMAN ✤

♀

TAURUS WOMAN:
SNAPSHOT

Trustworthy

Unrelenting

Home loving

Accountable

Enduring

It's ironic how the horned Bull is diametrically opposed to Venus, your soft and gentle ruling planet. At first, you come across as the perfect epitome of poise, charm and vigour, but gradually you reveal your innate fierceness and determination, which is intrinsic to your horned personality. People then awaken to the myriad facets of your colourful persona!

You are unrelenting, resolute and affectionate, although you exhibit abrupt mood swings and have strong Jekyll-and-Hyde tendencies. You rate truthfulness and fidelity highly, and if someone wants to witness your belligerent and imperious instincts, all they have to do is betray your trust. This triggers your 'bull' impulse and you will naturally charge at them.

Your Zodiac element of earth signifies how well grounded you are. You don't look down on others, and your keen awareness of your roots lends you a natural ability to connect with people from all walks of life, regardless of their class. For the more evolved Taurean, your earthy relative Virgo may find expression in your personality. This enables you to strive for perfection in any endeavour you put your mind to.

I have encountered countless Taurean women who are highly devoted to their dwelling. Your home is your castle and you painstakingly tend to every detail that needs attention. You shine as an exceptional hostess when visitors come knocking as you're born with the gift to nurture, love and comfort, not just your family and friends, but also perfect strangers.

You like to adhere to your own unique style of getting things done, much to the dismay of others who view you as inflexible and stiff. Allow room for adaptability, especially with your children, as they may become victims of your obsessive demand for perfection. Your intentions are good, but how you communicate and execute these intentions needs some attention. This same inflexibility and exacting attitude often springs up in the workplace. Nevertheless, your sincerity, perseverance and diligence remain unquestionable and outstanding.

A Little Goes a Long Way

You have an amazing ability to stretch your dollar, an ingenuity that can help you through gruelling financial times. But be wary of the excessive influence of Venus on your desire for sensual excess, and try to harmonise it with the practical realities of life.

You refrain from confrontations in relationships and prefer to walk silently away with grace. However, this doesn't lend happiness to your state of mind, as you bottle up all your emotions and carry them around like a heavy burden. Allow room for dialogue; the sooner you address your concerns verbally, the sooner you'll be able to shine as the woman you were potentially born to be.

Of all the Zodiac signs, Taurean women make the best mothers. Your children enjoy your overwhelming affection, encouragement and shielding influence. However, you can wind up overindulging them. Such extreme passion may have serious repercussions on your relationship with your partner, who will often be ignored.

TAURUS CHILD

Taurean children keep their parents perpetually on their toes! Their stubbornness doesn't thaw with words, rules and regulations alone. Parents will be forced to find a seamless blend of dexterity and ingenuity to keep them in check. Your biggest mission and challenge as a parent would be to tame your little one into doing things the way they're supposed to be done. On second thoughts, parents of Taurean kids might benefit from studying psychology to ease their stress while parenting!

The Taurus child prefers effortlessness and is forever cutting corners and jumping to shortcuts. Your key responsibility as a parent is to motivate them to go that extra mile by providing a sense of accomplishment. Drafting out a strict schedule and code of conduct will give them a blueprint to develop themselves instead of wandering off impulsively and aimlessly.

Taurean children bubble with natural affection and love because they were born under the sensual rays of Venus. They are at their happiest with endless cuddles, encouragement and emotional reliance, and could spend their lives blissfully bathing in your care. Give them your love and you'll be amazed at the degree of affection they throw back at you. They will be constantly finding ways to express their adoration of you.

Take care never to impose restrictions on their social group. It's crucial to remember that they breathe life into friendships and take great pleasure in the company of friends. Taurean children are also social bees whose sexual interests and activities need to be monitored, especially as they get older.

STAYING ACTIVE

Their enormous indolence can be conquered by a strict exercise and sport regimen. You will need to be alert and allow ample opportunity for physical training. Drag them off their cosy couches and into the sunshine so they can breathe fresh air and jiggle their bodies in a healthy and nourishing environment.

Another area that demands attention is your Taurean child's tendency to bully. Some less evolved children of this star sign tend to enjoy terrorising others, and your responsibility is to ensure that they respect others and don't always get their way. This could be even more difficult to achieve if yours is an only child. If you're not mindful of these inherent tendencies, they can be spoilt in no time and suffer the repercussions. Friendship, after all, thrives best when one cares and shares. They need to know this, so make sure you teach them this valuable lesson.

On the whole, Taurean children adore their families and are innately affectionate and caring. You can put your absolute faith in their ability to complete a job as they respond well to order. Try to assign duties and tasks to them from an early age. This will become an ingrained habit and prevent lethargy and sluggishness from creeping into their character.

TAURUS LOVER

As one of the most dependable and committed of the zodiac signs, you rate reliability as imperative to a successful relationship. You blossom best in the comfort of sincerity and openness. In the absence of these essential requirements, you refuse to open up and shy away from surrendering your heart.

You often reach stalemates in your life, particularly in relationships. You may cling to a past romance with the same intensity as if it were a current relationship. Relying on time to heal unpleasant wounds may not be the best option as it'll restrict you from taking the plunge again. Of course, you long for someone special, so sever the emotional chains around you and embrace the limitless possibilities instead.

You are as possessive and overprotective in love as you are with some of your material belongings. Try not to stifle your partner or succumb to jealousy or it will damage your relationship with negativity and mistrust. You must rest your belief in your partner and foster a spirit of independence towards her or him. This simple act of trust and liberty can be beneficial for your relationship, and your partner will be more willing to reciprocate and less prone to wander.

A Prudential Partner

Financial stability is important to you, which is why you prefer a monetarily sound partner. Your search is definitely not for a multimillionaire. Rather, you sail with ease knowing your partner enjoys a steady income and is prudent with expenses and savings. This simple security is what you desire.

Although you are honest, you could be uncomplicated and upfront in the way you do this. As a result, people may also find you excessively honest! Providing detailed reasoning for your opinions will stand you in good stead, especially when you feel incapable of speaking up and your relationship is at risk of going into shut-down mode.

What your relationships truly require is compromise. Pour every ounce of yourself into being supportive and flexible. These traits don't come naturally to you, so you need to inculcate them. Your relationships bloom best amidst excitement and spontaneity, not control or anxiety. A positive shift in your attitude is all that's needed for sparking a relationship.

Once you're comfortably ensconced in a relationship, the sensual elements of your nature come into sight. When this happens, you immerse yourself in the pleasurable aspects of that feeling. Be wary of getting carried away or overindulging such tendencies. Your relationship flourishes best in moderation.

In short, your relationships go beyond simple attraction. You need to feel snug and warm. You also need to know that your significant other is as keen as you are and that your temperaments complement each other. For you, Taurus, love is for keeps, particularly if you're in your 30s or older. One night stands and flings definitely don't enthrall you.

TAURUS FRIEND

You take great pride in your choice of friends and select carefully before committing to them. You prefer quality to quantity. You also enjoy friendship with people who exhibit good taste in the way they dress, the lifestyle they lead and their general demeanour. Superficial people don't even get to first base, and anyone with an ego would do well to leave it at the door.

Friendship with powerful people attracts you, especially if they are happy to share this power with you. You are extremely dependable, and this is one of the things your friends like about you. They will look to you for guidance and stability, and even in times of trouble you will be there for them.

TRUSTWORTHY TAURUS

You are trustworthy, not given to sudden changes of plans, and your friends always know what to expect. With you, Taurus, nothing comes out of left field.

When meeting someone for the first time, you will play your cards close to your chest until you work out who they are and how they relate to you. This is one of the reasons why you build good, strong friendships, albeit slowly.

You can be jealous, Taurus, and not always on a proven basis. You do not like signs of weakness, physical or emotional, and can be quite direct about it. You, of course, see yourself as strong as a bull, and this perceived weakness in others is a real turn-off for you.

It is unlikely that you will forget a friend's birthday and you will probably plan something in advance so you don't miss their special occasion. This is a trait that your friends really appreciate about you. When purchasing a gift for someone you love, you spend a lot of time considering what they would like so they are happy with what they receive.

Taureans do not follow the crowd in changing fads and fashion; they develop their own style. You have inbuilt good taste and know exactly what suits you and your personality.

You love to entertain and your friends will enjoy sharing these occasions with you. Social occasions are a way of having lively discussions, exchanging ideas and sharing food and drink from faraway places.

Loyal and devoted, you do not take friendship lightly, and you hate to lose a friend. However, it must be said that you hold grudges for a long time and remember every wrongdoing in boring detail. Lighten up!

TAURUS ENEMY

Taurus can be remarkably unwearied by rivals, and they can keep disagreements and confrontations at bay. However, they are also horned bulls who, when provoked, can disrupt all semblance of harmony. They don't like to be treated unfairly, so if you have any such designs, brace yourself to encounter a raging bull charging at you at full speed.

Taurus doesn't easily identify himself/herself as a potential enemy. They have a knack for keeping their emotions under wraps and won't even give you a whiff of the grudges they may nurse against you. You could spend every waking moment in their company, oblivious to the negativity lurking deep within them. However, the Bull is not a cow! Their containment never lasts as they're bound to explode. With a Taurus enemy, it's not a matter of 'if', but 'when'.

Because of their tendency to steer clear of confrontations, it does take a considerable amount of cornering to rile them up. But when you begin to witness your Taurus enemy rising to reveal the darkness within, you'll probably marvel at how they managed to contain such a blaze of anger for so long! Being ruled by the Bull it is a warning. When they are taken over by their anger, they pierce you with their horns and toss over anyone else who crosses their path. Because Taurus can be extremely possessive of their belongings, and protective of the people they love, even a minor misconduct is likely to arouse feelings of jealousy and riotous anger.

In personal circumstances where Taurus is wronged by a friend, one can witness the same fury described above. If you're on the receiving end of this, you'll be left traumatised and wondering how someone so meek and mild could unleash this violent avalanche of anger and beastliness.

In a nutshell, Taurus has zero tolerance for unfair treatment, and never forgives or forgets an insult or misconduct. In fact, they could take years to forgive someone they regard as an enemy.

TAURUS

AT HOME

YOU ONLY LIVE ONCE, BUT IF YOU
DO IT RIGHT, ONCE IS ENOUGH.

Mae West

HOME FRONT

Taurus is driven by the need for security. Because you desire shelter and protection, having a warm, comfortable and secure home is a significant component of your overall wellbeing. To top it off, family plays a pivotal role in experiencing a heightened degree of confidence and happiness in life. Truly, your home is your castle.

At home, you work to create a gentle and relaxed atmosphere that offers a perfect setting for letting your hair down and embracing the company of others. Your home exudes effortless calm that makes even solitude appear refreshing. Being an earth sign, you derive immense pleasure from decorating your interiors with garden greens and fragrant blossoms that add warmth to your Taurean lifestyle.

The Perfect Oasis

On a perfect Saturday afternoon, you can be found comfortably ensconced on a sunny porch, the aromatic smell of coffee beans tickling your senses, pampered by the sheer simplicity of having cookies, roses and your favorite book by your side.

Taureans are masters in the kitchen and exude both a love for cooking and a great appetite for it too! Your kitchen is well stocked with fresh, earthy ingredients, including herbs and possibly even your own garden-grown vegetables. For you, cooking is not about culinary skill; it's an expression of your womanhood and regard for your family.

When it comes to décor, your style is graceful with soft fabrics and luxurious curtains and carpets adorning your living space. You prefer a traditional or ornate look with a luxurious touch rather than anything outlandish. Furniture, tapestry and colour are your primary concerns when doing up your home. Pastels and shades that don't scream for attention are the ones you pick, and you're inclined to a subdued style of lighting, all of which complement your Taurean temperament perfectly. In any case, what you desire is a sparkling, spotless home where things are just as they're meant to be. You hate it when someone restructures a setting you are used to.

You relax best in solitude. This is a requirement, especially if you lead a frantic work life. The physical setting of such a space is vital to help you revitalise yourself. You need a warm and comfortable room to stretch your legs, connect with your inner being and realign yourself.

Taureans are incredibly proud of their homes and love showing them off. Keeping up with the Joneses may become a problem for some of you born under this sign. But because you are cautious with money, you have a flair for making your house look a lot more ostentatious and expensive than it really is.

KARMA, LUCK AND MEDITATION

You're not born with luck, nor does it come your way. Taureans usually toil with grit and fortitude to earn their good fortune. Rely on your insight and labour to taste true success instead of resting on someone else's laurels. Even if you are offered a dream undertaking, you don't necessarily trust that success will slide easily into your lap.

Your past karma and fortune is governed by Saturn. This means that the rewards of your karmic fruits won't manifest until much later in life. The luck you obtain is usually due to your immense hard work and the challenges others don't normally experience. The influence of Saturn on your life is tremendously compelling.

Virgo and Mercury determine your future karma. Mercury is an auspicious planet and indicates a happy future, provided you don't stifle your emotions. Allow easy dialogue to flow forth, and if you work to ensure productive communication, you will naturally attract favourable vibrations that will bring you success, wealth and prosperity in relationships.

'I possess' is your life phrase. Strip yourself of all the material possessions you've acquired and get in touch with who you really are. Once you are able to separate the reality of your existence from the fleeting happiness of material wealth, you will activate your spiritual mind and value your chattels so much more. This is ideal if you want to experience peace of mind and true joy.

Wednesday, Friday and Saturday are opportune days to attempt emotional healing and self-advancement. Invest some time in exploring your hidden quirkiness and doing something spontaneous you wouldn't normally do. Challenging your own limits can augment your fortune.

Lucky Days

Your luckiest days are Wednesday, Friday and Saturday.

Lucky Numbers

Lucky numbers for Taurus include the following. You may wish to experiment with these in Lotto and other games of chance.

6, 15, 24, 33, 42, 51

5, 14, 23, 32, 41, 50

8, 17, 26, 35, 44, 53

Destiny Years

The most significant years in your life are likely to be 6, 15, 24, 33, 42, 51, 60, 78 and 87.

HEALTH, WELLBEING AND DIET

You are naturally blessed with resilient healthiness, although you're not quite as lucky when diet comes into play. Of course, the two go hand in glove. You flaunt a robust physique with a natural ability to withstand extremes in climate and environment, and your stamina is unconquerable.

The reason you are 'not quite lucky' with regards to your diet is due to your tendency to overindulge. Your foremost goal is to moderate your diet, drinking and lifestyle, thereby allowing your health to improve. If you pay a little attention to how your body responds to certain types of food, your constitution will stand to benefit hugely. For instance, Taurus inherently has a sweet tooth. You are drawn to all that's rich, saccharine and luscious. As a result, you muddle up a variety of flavours that disagree internally. Ignoring your digestive system in favour of overindulgence will dramatically impact your physical vigour.

Refrain from sugar, candy, cakes and other calorific victuals. Choose lean, white meat as opposed to heavy, red meat and other animal products. This small modification can help boost your energy levels.

Taurus rules the throat, mouth, neck and face. These body parts have an intrinsic potential to cause infirmity at some point in your life. Ensure frequent examination of your tonsils, thyroid and parathyroid.

FINANCE FINESSE

You take money quite seriously and regard it as a measure of your happiness and contentment in life. Financial security for Taurus is what water is to fish— they'd die without it.

Taurus is an earth sign and a natural ruler of the financial sector of the Zodiac. This indicates why you value material resourcefulness and stability for overall wellbeing. It is also the reason why Taureans place immense emphasis on securing a sound financial base from an early age. They toil towards building future security, without which they feel unable to reach out to their loved ones or pursue their chosen career.

This paranoia can assume aberrant proportions and compromise your relationships or emotional balance. You must control your need for financial gratification, as your relationships will be one of the first casualties. Try not to overemphasise monetary assets or get caught up in outward displays. After all, these are only accessories to real happiness. Security is important, but not at the cost of relationships you treasure.

TAURUS
AT WORK

BE YOURSELF; EVERYONE ELSE
IS ALREADY TAKEN.

Oscar Wilde

TAURUS CAREER

Without the foundational support of Taurus, a business may be likely to fall to bits. Taureans may be slow and steady, but they accomplish even the most menial of tasks with excellence. Disciplined and responsible, Taurus possess the qualities that any business needs to succeed.

Taurus abides by exceptional work ethics and is respected for this reason. They work with an acute sense of pride and responsibility, and reveal this quality even as homemakers or domestic help. They perform each task with perfection, treating their work as an expression of care and nurturing.

If you are an employer and require a quicker turnaround, perhaps you'd benefit from a compromise with your Taurean employee. Rest assured of the quality of the output; they will bring you a finished product with no errors, for they hate making mistakes. They let their work do the talking, leaving you hugely satisfied at the end of it. They always take pride in their work—and it shows.

Stress Alert

Your greatest challenge, Taurus, is deadline-related stress, which compels you to work beyond your comfort level. If you have a Taurus co-worker or employee, respect their pace and you don't strangle them with your own terms or tempo.

❧

Taureans are best suited to a practical, systematised style of work. Potential occupations would include real estate, building, interior design, architecture and other construction industries. Financial and banking sectors, along with investment portfolios, are zones that can be carved into fine career options for Taurus.

Your ruling planet is Venus, and because Venus exhibits strong creative qualities, you can safely explore beauty, fashion, arts, film and dance as promising career avenues. To add to this, your Zodiac element, earth, allows you to successfully turn gardening, handicrafts and horticulture into booming careers as well.

Luckily for you, your career planet Uranus has a lot to offer. It bestows you with perpetual strength and open-mindedness to attempt something distinctive and progressive. Even though you're inclined towards traditional careers, you may find yourself drawn to modern technologies.

TAURUS BOSS

Surrendering yourself to the working style of a Taurus boss will be the best possible course of action. They call the shots and decide the rules, regardless of where you were a big a player in the past. In short, it's either their way or the highway! A typical Taurus boss is an imposing figure, in control of his/her emotions. They demand a conservative, peaceful and regimented atmosphere to function comfortably and fulfil their responsibilities.

Taurean bosses perform best in a simple and comfortable work environment as opposed to a palatial set up. If you fancy this style at work, you'll get along well with your Taurean boss. Taurus employers are tolerant but also particular about the way they like things to be done. They prefer to be unhurried and precise rather than rush to a conclusion. If you're the employee, try and sync your timelines with your Taurean boss's requirements. Remember, they are in no rush to meet yours, and will make you wait until they make up their minds. Dealing with this could be quite challenging.

A Taurus boss will have every minute of their business life chalked out with extreme precision. Not only do they adhere to a schedule for themselves, they expect others to abide by it too. They don't allow room for surprises, so be prepared to give them adequate notice of your time out. Any delay on your part may awaken the Taurean Bull from its slumber, and that is not good news for you. It happens rarely, but when the Bull charges, erupting with anger, all hell breaks loose.

Taurean bosses are as stubborn as they are faithful to their employees. They are driven by a sense of responsibility to support their staff under all circumstances, more so if the employee exhibits an equal measure of loyalty to them. They display the same devotion to a business as they do to a marriage, and they understand that a good working relationship is beneficial for achieving mutual goals.

TAURUS EMPLOYEE

Your qualities as a Taurus make you an excellent employee as you are supremely steadfast and reliable, pushing yourself to excel beyond the limits of the job. However, if you're an employer, you may need to understand few intricate details about your Taurus employee if you wish to benefit from hiring them.

By now you will be aware of Taurus's need for an organised environment. If you happen to employ one, draft a structured schedule to optimise their performance. Also, they work tirelessly to complete a task and may require additional time to achieve a fine result. But thrusting a clock in their face to meet a deadline may backfire on you and result in a compromised output.

NON-CONFRONTATIONAL TAURUS

Taureans prefer to steer clear of confrontations, even at crucial moments. They may be on the brink of exploding with anger at being treated unfairly, but they'll rarely speak up unless their opinion is solicited. When it is, expect an honest response.

Taureans have a natural inclination towards comfortable, relaxed and welcoming settings. This can make them turn insipid and sterile spaces into resplendent work zones. They don't rely on systematised design and prefer putting flowers in the lobby or hanging a painting in the hallway. They ensure their office pulsates with warmth and friendliness and find inexpensive yet colourful ways to achieve this aim!

Taurus is resistant to change, so if an employer provides satisfactory remuneration and reasonable working conditions, they won't desert them. Taureans are known for dependability, punctuality and sincere work ethics, which is everything that an employer desires. But you must never push them to compromise their ethics or suffocate them with undue stress or it will jeopardise your relationship with them forever. You will have to find your own way to fix inefficiencies, chaotic routines and instability, as your Taurus employee will be of no help.

Once they commit themselves to a job, Taureans are completely with you. Regardless of how they feel about you as their employer, they revere and respect the position of authority you hold.

PROFESSIONAL
RELATIONSHIPS:
BEST AND WORST

BEST PAIRING:
TAURUS AND CAPRICORN

You enjoy a special affinity with the Zodiac sign of Capricorn, be it personal, professional or financial. The elemental similarity of earth underpins this relationship and yields extraordinary results in any business endeavour.

A Great Match

As a Taurus, you're committed to financial security and a job that gives you creative contentment. These are key ingredients in your life and without them you'd be miserable. Luckily, Capricorn offers you much of what you seek in life, making this a hugely gratifying professional union.

Like you, Capricorns are not driven by the urgency of getting results. They exhibit a conservative approach and long-term vision. They display a remarkable ability to stand unhurried and panic-free, even in the face of stressful circumstances. Clear-headed, they focus on their ambitions and steadfastly work towards them on their own terms.

Capricorn is ruled by Saturn, a planet that has an affinity with the revolutionary sign of Aquarius. Simply put, with Aquarius as a sign of finance, Capricorn possesses astute ways of making money through grit and hard work.

You also have a similar ideology of concentrating on quality rather than speed, and derive immense pride from the eventual output. Regardless of whether Capricorn is your employer or employee, you two will enjoy mutual respect and admiration. Capricorn is quick to grasp your chain of thought, and they will allow flexibility in your schedule to ensure optimal productivity.

You both share the ability to be realistic as well as financially cautious. Neither of you is a spendthrift unless you feel confident about your financial grounding. Until you secure such a foundation, you will self-sacrifice and manage economically until you can reward yourselves for a job well done. Once accomplished, you justify all the past frugality by buying nothing short of the best.

WORST PAIRING:
TAURUS AND AQUARIUS

Aquarius and Taurus stand diametrically opposed due to the influence of their respective ruling planets. While you are ruled by the conservative and unhurried Venus, Aquarius challenges the limits of tradition and convention. Right from the start, your equation with Aquarius will be marked with anxiety, confrontation and apprehension.

Aquarius also nurses monetary concerns, though not the way you do. Their risk-taking capacity rates high, with some uncalculated moves due to their highly unconventional vision of life and its possibilities. You, Taurus, are bereft of this confidence, and you cling to the tried and tested instead. This alone suggests the multitude of flare ups that will occur between you, with each attempting to secure the upper hand.

Even if you succeed in establishing a seemingly comfortable working relationship, you are persistently assailed by a fear of your Aquarian partner's daring approach to life. You do not respect each other's views, and you gradually discern this reality through perpetual disagreement.

Amusingly, the dissimilarity between you and Aquarius is a result of the similarity in the fixity of your star signs! This means an inability on both sides to adjust to the needs and circumstances of the other.

TAURUS

IN LOVE

NO ONE CAN MAKE YOU FEEL INFERIOR
WITHOUT YOUR CONSENT.

Eleanor Roosevelt

ROMANTIC
COMPATIBILITY

Are you compatible with your current partner, lover or friend? Astrology reveals a great deal about people and their relationships through their star signs. In this chapter, I'd like to show you how to better appreciate your strengths and challenges using Sun sign compatibility.

The Sun reflects your drive, willpower and personality. The essential qualities of two star signs blend like two pure colours producing an entirely new colour. Relationships, similarly, produce their own emotional colours when two people interact. The following is a general guide to your romantic prospects with others and how, by knowing the astrological 'colour' of each other, the art of love can help you create a masterpiece.

The Star Sign Compatibility for Love and Friendship table rates your chance as a percentage of general compatibility, while the Horoscope Compatibility table summarises the reasons why. Each star sign combination is followed by the elements of those star signs and the result of their combining. For instance, Aries is a fire sign and Aquarius is an air sign and this combination produces a lot of 'hot air'. Air feeds fire and fire warms air. In fact, fire requires air. However, not all air and fire combinations work.

When reading the following, I ask you to remember that no two star signs are ever *totally* incompatible. With effort and compromise, even the most 'difficult' astrological matches can work. Don't close your mind to the full range of life's possibilities! Learning about each other and ourselves is the most important facet of astrology.

Good luck in your search for love, and may the stars shine upon you in 2014!

STAR SIGN COMPATIBILITY FOR LOVE AND FRIENDSHIP (PERCENTAGES)

	Aries	Taurus	Gemini	Cancer	Leo	Virgo	Libra	Scorpio	Sagittarius	Capricorn	Aquarius	Pisces
Aries	60	65	65	65	90	45	70	80	90	50	55	65
Taurus	60	70	70	80	70	90	75	85	50	95	80	85
Gemini	70	70	75	60	80	75	90	60	75	50	90	50
Cancer	65	80	60	75	70	75	60	95	55	45	70	90
Leo	90	70	80	70	85	75	65	75	95	45	70	75
Virgo	45	90	75	75	75	70	80	85	70	95	50	70
Libra	70	75	90	60	65	80	80	85	80	85	95	50
Scorpio	80	85	60	95	75	85	85	90	80	65	60	95
Sagittarius	90	50	75	55	95	70	80	85	85	55	60	75
Capricorn	50	95	50	45	45	95	85	65	55	85	70	85
Aquarius	55	80	90	70	70	50	95	60	60	70	80	55
Pisces	65	85	50	90	75	70	50	95	75	85	55	80

HOROSCOPE COMPATIBILITY
FOR TAURUS

Taurus with		Romance/Sexual
Aries		Amorous and tender affair; tumultuous from time to time
Taurus		Doting and sensual match; star twins
Gemini		Terrific friends and lovers; Gemini rouses Taurus
Cancer		You have a calming effect on the temperamental Cancer
Leo		Electrifying in the bedroom, though both of you are still rigid
Virgo		Most remarkable Zodiac combo; a promising romance

	Friendship		Professional
✔	Enjoyable, though Aries tends to dictate	✔	A fine combination; Aries is the engine and Taurus is the chassis
✔	Mutual interests, but could deteriorate without inventiveness	✔	A fitting financial match
✔	Fascinating interaction; Gemini demands intellectual inspiration	✔	Ingenious match that energises the aspirations and ambitions of both
✘	Constant monitoring is vital as Cancer is too hypersensitive for you	✔	Cancer benefits most from this match
✔	Possibly motivating for both, but Leos can be easily provoked	✔	Powerful association that can generate success
✔	Intimate, though Virgo is fault-finding	✔	Good exploratory match balanced by Taurus's vigilance and financial prudence

Taurus with		Romance/Sexual
Libra		Sexual interests match, though Libra could be excessively weighty
Scorpio		Awesome attraction and likely to last, but assailed by intense emotional fluctuations
Sagittarius		Utter mismatch; mutually frustrating
Capricorn		Sexually comforting for both; you turn them on
Aquarius		Progressive Aquarius may seem eccentric and volatile, leaving you baffled and wordless
Pisces		Pisces adores Taurus unreservedly, but Pisces can be too idealistic

Friendship		Professional	
✔	Libra is a good friend, but allow them space and let go of your overprotectiveness	✔	Let go of the past strains; Libra offers refreshing ideas that could benefit you
✔	Largely a marvellous friendship, though Scorpio demands excessive attention	✘	Obstinacy at its worst; an absolute refusal to acknowledge what the other may bring to the table
✔	Convivial, thrilling match; an adventurous combo	✘	Sagittarius stands to benefit hugely from Taurus, but not the other way around
✔	Predictable Capricorn puts you at ease; you enjoy common interests	✔	Remarkable team work in which much can be achieved; a triumphant partnership
✔	Aquarius stimulates Taurus to challenge their emotional confines and think outside the box	✔	Imaginative Aquarius can help you forge a new career path
✔	Wonderful friendship, but it can hit philosophical snags	✔	Pisces provides sound financial understanding and viable options you want to pursue

TAURUS
PARTNERSHIPS

Taurus + Aries

Aries motivates you while you bring stability to their lives. You're practical and offer concrete, temperate guidance due to your security-conscious attitude. While you both enjoy a delightful sexual relationship, be wary of power issues that may taint your relationship.

Taurus + Taurus

You find solace in this union as it satisfies your need for control, guidance and security. You complete each other beautifully in this respect. You share mutual inclinations towards wealth, creating a relaxed abode and having a flourishing family life. The only caveat is that you're both extremely susceptible to becoming couch potatoes.

Taurus + Gemini

Gemini electrifies your imagination, which can benefit you. Your sexual compatibility rates very high as your ruling planets enjoy tremendous affability. While you are fascinated by Gemini's inquisitive and imaginative mind, they are attracted to your sensuality.

Taurus + Cancer

The warmth and understanding you extend to each other heralds a wonderful astrological compatibility. You share common life goals with each other, desiring long-term financial security and a contented domestic life. Both of you demonstrate feminine traits of care and compassion, which trickle into your sexual relationship and make it satisfying.

Taurus + Leo

There is a very compelling sexual bond between you and Leo, but you move at a measured and restrained pace. Allow time for the two of you to deepen your fondness beyond the physical. You are both obstinate and opinionated. Only when you dig deeper will you discover a meaningful and lasting bond.

Taurus + Virgo

Hailing from a common earth sign, both of you shine as ideal soul mates. While most react adversely to the fault-finding habits of Virgo, you can handle them impeccably. Splendid attraction and a faultless amalgamation of minds make this a win-win situation. Lovemaking is unrestrained and, many times, cathartic for both.

Taurus + Libra

Although you're born under the same planetary rulership, there exists a disparity between your respective styles. Libra demands a higher degree of motivation than what you're prepared to give, especially at the start of the relationship when you, Taurus, need time to open up. The most constructive way to foster this relationship is to communicate from early on and make an effort to voice your thoughts.

Taurus + Scorpio

Your love story seems straight out of a film, and it shows just how wonderfully opposites can attract! However, your reality with Scorpio is beset with conflicting ideologies that both of you refuse to let go of, which only leads you to a perpetual impasse. Apart from these psychological and emotional differences, you both enjoy a delightful physical attraction.

Taurus + Sagittarius

Sagittarius is way too uninhibited and spontaneous for your devotedly structured ways. Their inability to remain steadfast in a relationship happens to be your key grievance, while you are excessively loyal. At the same time, verbal interaction with Sagittarius goes nowhere due to their nagging persistence, which aggravates your ability to communicate. Astrologically, your ruling planets are not compatible.

Taurus + Capricorn

As with Virgo, you share the sign of earth with Capricorn as well. This is a remarkably great match. As a couple, you share a similar vision and direction, and your temperaments faultlessly complement each other to bring out the best. This is a balanced relationship where you feel mutually supported. Sexually satisfying, Capricorn's traditional outlook is in perfect sync with yours.

Taurus + Aquarius

The progressive mannerisms of Aquarius leave you utterly unnerved, robbing you of a potential relationship. Only if you loosen up and accept their distinctive opinions and lifestyle choices could there be a fruitful journey for you. You enjoy the sexual gratification, but only temporarily. Your conventionality can only bear so much of Aquarius's quirky and eccentric style.

Taurus + Pisces

This happens to be one of the better combinations of the Zodiac spectrum as you are both blessed with love and care right from the start. You exhibit a mutual fondness and thoughtfulness, and Pisces supports you wholeheartedly in every possible way, even in the bedroom. Overall, this affinity makes for an impressive partnership.

PLATONIC RELATIONSHIPS: BEST AND WORST

BEST PAIRING: TAURUS AND PISCES

The revelation that Pisces is your ideal platonic match may render you utterly flabbergasted. You are realistic, unassuming and heavily reliant on financial security, while your Piscean counterpart is serenely spiritual and unmaterialistic. But what you may opine as an ineffectual match is actually your greatest benefit. Pisces is the 11th sign to Taurus, signifying intimate companionship, which lends a seamless balance to your temperament.

Astrologically, this is an exceptional combination. Notwithstanding Piscean's oversensitive disposition, you're amazingly adept at reaching out to their feminine side, regardless of their sex. On the other hand, your inflexibility bends when rubbed against the Piscean temperament, which encourages them to stand firm in their opinions as well. These mutually harmonising factors enable you to cultivate a relationship of empathy and trust.

Your tendency to be excessively money-oriented exercises a wonderful influence on your materialistically naive Piscean friend. Conversely, Pisces alleviates your obsession with financial security and encourages you to be more spiritual and gain profound insights into yourself instead. Because they reveal the same dedication in their own lives, you're able to give meaning to these expressions of spirituality, which were otherwise unknown to you. Karmically, you combine to teach each other valuable lessons in life. Some Pisceans seem to wander in a vacuum, seeking an anchor that they find in you, and they, in turn, stir your curiosity.

....

GENEROUS PISCES

Your temperament rekindles self-confidence in your Piscean friends, and they like to silently serve your individual needs without screaming for centre stage or expecting the same intensity from you. Try not to abuse the generosity they extend. Once gone, you will never be able to salvage this otherwise perfect friendship.

....

WORST PAIRING:
TAURUS AND LEO

You're both exceptionally opinionated and headed for a catastrophic platonic relationship. While your ruling planets are not perfectly positioned in the Zodiac spectrum, there exists the possibility of favourable attraction that lends buoyancy and cheerfulness in personal and social engagements.

Your first acquaintance with Leo is likely to trigger happy emotions, as they're ruled by the bright and warm Sun. They also exhibit a vivacious sense of humour and outgoingness that naturally draws you to them. Silently, you may be envious of how oblivious they are to societal judgments and notions.

Governed by Venus, Taurus is naturally calm and sociable, but they may not quite at peace with themselves as Leo would be. This is the point where Leo can inspire a greater sense of self-confidence in you.

As both of you are immovable signs of the Zodiac, you are obstinacy personified, and you remain steadfastly glued to your own ways of thinking. When this happens, your initial admiration towards Leo begins to wane, and you wonder whether their overwhelming confidence was in fact a reservoir of deep-seated insecurities.

SEXUAL RELATIONSHIPS: BEST AND WORST

BEST PAIRING:
TAURUS AND VIRGO

Three key constituents determine the compatibility between star signs. Firstly, the elemental composition of each star sign, which happens to be earth for both Taurus and Virgo. This ensures compatibility, steadiness and contentment in the relationship. The second component deals with the amity between planets that rule you. Venus dominates Taurus while Mercury presides over Virgo, both incredibly friendly in astrological terms. This enhances the potential for a pleasing sexual relationship.

The third component pertains to the physical proximity or distance between two star signs. Virgo falls in the fifth zone to your Sun sign. The fifth zone pulsates with romance, love affairs, imagination and offspring. This means that you extend natural attraction towards each other, both romantically and sexually. As a result, I deem you highly sexually compatible!

You easily identify with Virgos, as you relate to their qualities of spotlessness, practicality and service. Virgo echoes a similar sentiment about you, and from the outset the two of you enjoy mutual admiration and regard. All these qualities culminate to create a hugely satisfying, rewarding and liberating sexual relationship.

Sexual Fulfilment

Virgo's keen awareness of your needs is another plus that allows you to experience sexual fulfilment. You are definitely blessed to experience such earnestness and candour in bed, Taurus!

Virgo is inherently critical, but your realistic influence pacifies this tendency. Interestingly, your diligence and precision in executing tasks helps obliterate Virgo's natural apprehension; you rarely give them a chance to fault find with you. Even if they somehow manage to pick on you, you display an uncanny calmness that is devoid of the usual vehemence you show other star signs. This helps mitigate confrontations in your relationship.

All these qualities signify a demonstrative, sensual and light-hearted sexual union. If the past had you shying away from inventiveness in bed, Virgo encourages you to explore unimaginable possibilities! Notwithstanding the virginal tendencies of Virgo with other star signs, the two of you create magic together and take physical contact to another level!

WORST PAIRING:
TAURUS AND SAGITTARIUS

With your supremely divergent and conflicting personalities, I am at a loss when it comes to this sexual union. To cut a long story short, you will find yourself asking, 'Should I even bother?' But I think I've spilled the beans before offering an in-depth elucidation.

Initially, Taurus, you can struggle with voicing your feelings. To be yourself, it's imperative to establish a level of comfort with your partner where your concerns and thoughts can be revealed without fear of judgment. Sagittarius does exactly the opposite. They blissfully misconstrue this trait of yours and accuse you of emotional incongruity.

They harbour these erroneous misconceptions based upon their own experience and the fact that the Jupiter-ruled Sagittarius is unguarded, buoyant and at times incredibly overbearing and unsympathetic. Taurus and Sagittarius are also entirely different when it comes to style, life, direction or even long-term vision. How can their bedroom relationship be any different?

Taurus can be accused of being extravagantly pleasure-seeking, and their penchant for sensuality also manifests during sex. Though Sagittarians are also quite indulgent, there is a definite distinction between you. You may initially revel in each other's company during your night romps and pillow fights, but watch out as you both have different motivations.

Sagittarius exhibits a carefree personality and enjoys the excesses of life and lust. You definitely don't come from such a world, Taurus. Though you enjoy profligacy, your fixed Zodiac sign also indicates a high degree of faithfulness, which your Sagittarian partner may not be able to give. Not only does this tendency unnerve you, their incessant prodding amplifies your dissatisfaction. While you require comfort and openness of communication, the lack of patience and cornering by your Sagittarian counterpart pushes you back into your shell, and the vicious circle continues.

Though Sagittarians clearly enjoy your amorous and adoring attention, they insist on having the liberty to explore other possibilities in life. If that's the case, make sure you clearly define your beliefs at the outset, letting them know that an open relationship is simply out of the question.

QUIZ: HAVE YOU FOUND YOUR PERFECT MATCH?

Do you dare take the following quiz to see how good a lover you are? Remember, although the truth sometimes hurts, it's the only way to develop your relationship skills.

We are all searching for our soul mate: that idyllic romantic partner who will fulfill our wildest dreams of love and emotional security. Unfortunately, finding true love isn't easy. Sometimes, even when you are in a relationship, you can't help but wonder whether or not your partner is right for you. How can you possibly know?

It's essential to question your relationships and work on ways to improve your communication and overall happiness. When meeting someone new, it's also a good idea to study their intentions and read between the lines. In the first instance, when your hormones are taking over, it's easy to get carried away and forget some of the basic principles of what makes a relationship endure.

You're probably wondering where to start. Are you in a relationship at the moment? Are you looking for love but finding it difficult to choose between two or more people? Are you simply not able to meet someone at all? Well, there are some basic questions you can ask yourself to discover how suited you and your partner are. And if you don't have a partner, consider your previous relationships to improve your chances next time.

The following quiz is a serious attempt to take an honest look at yourself and see whether or not your relationships are on track. Don't rush through this questionnaire. Think carefully about your practical day-to-day life and whether or not the relationship you are in genuinely fulfils your needs and the other person's needs. There's no point being in a relationship if you're gaining no satisfaction out of it.

Now, if you aren't completely satisfied with the results you get, don't give up! It's an opportunity for you to work on the relationship and improve things. But you mustn't let your ego get in the way as that's not going to get you anywhere.

Taurus, you're a loyal individual in all relationships, especially romantic ones. You need a partner who can offer you security, love and support. Finding the right person is an important key to your future romantic happiness. Below is your checklist to ascertain whether he or she is the right one for you.

Scoring System:

Yes = 1 point

No = 0 points

- ❓ Does he or she admire and respect you?

- ❓ Does he or she make you proud?

- ❓ Does he or she exude the willingness to listen to your side of the story?

- ❓ Does he or she adjust her- or himself to your opinions?

- ❓ Does he or she cherish you and demonstrate it?

- ❓ Does he or she support you in times of stress?

- ❓ Is he or she happy to stay home and enjoy family life?

- ❓ Is he or she a hard worker?

- ❓ Does he or she provide you financial security?

- ❓ Does he or she make you the centre of attention?

- ❓ Does he or she cook for you?

- ❓ Is he or she sensitive, tactile and romantic?

- ❓ Is he or she willing to give you space when you require it?

- ❓ Is he or she faithful to you?

- ❓ Does he or she sexually satisfy you?

- ❓ Was he or she born under the signs of Virgo, Capricorn, Pisces or Cancer?

Have you jotted down your answers honestly? If you're finding it hard to come up with the right answers, let your intuition help you and try not to force the answer. Of course there's no point in turning a blind eye to treatment that is less than acceptable, otherwise you're not going to have a realistic appraisal of your prospects with your current love interest. Here are the possible points you can score:

8 to 16

A good match. This shows that you and your partner enjoy a healthy understanding and reciprocate just the way you need. However, this is no reason to be slack out of complacency. You must continue working and improving your bond to make it shine more brilliantly than it does now.

5 to 7

Half-hearted prospect. You need to work hard at building your relationship and engage in honest self-examination. It takes two to tango, so you're obviously aware that you are both to blame. Go through each question systematically, making notes of areas where you can improve yourself. Undertaking this self-examination will guarantee favourable shifts in your relationship. But if things don't improve in spite of the effort, it may be time for you to rethink your future with this person.

♥☠ 0 to 4

On the rocks. I'm sorry to say that this relationship is completely devoid of basic mutual respect and understanding. It's likely that the two of you argue a lot. Your partner is also completely oblivious to your emotional needs. This is the perfect example of incompatibility. The big question is: Why are you still with this person? This requires some brutally honest self-examination on your part. You need to see whether there is some inherent insecurity within you that is causing you to hold onto something that has outgrown its use in your life. You may also be a victim of fear, which is preventing you from letting go of a relationship that no longer fulfils your needs. Self-honesty is the key here. You need to make some rather bold sacrifices to attract the right partner into your life.

2014
YEARLY OVERVIEW

LIVE AS IF YOU WERE TO DIE TOMORROW.
LEARN AS IF YOU WERE TO LIVE FOREVER.

Mahatma Gandhi

KEY EXPERIENCES

There comes a time in our lives, Taurus, when our values are completely out of sync with our lifestyle. When this happens, incredible changes take place. This is exactly what is going to happen to you in the coming 12 months.

In your horoscope, a cluster of planets astrologers call a Stellium, which includes Venus, Mercury, Pluto, the Sun and the Moon, congregate in your ninth zone of the higher mind, philosophy and morale values. The tough aspect from Mars and Uranus, as well as Jupiter at the commencement of the year, also set the trend for what should be some challenging changes, but if you embrace these changes, it will be an exciting year.

The most intense area of your life will be your romantic involvements, as shown by Saturn in your marital zone throughout the whole of 2014. With the beneficial influence of Jupiter in this sector, however, any trials and tribulations you experience will ultimately be an extraordinary learning curve for you, bringing deep insights into yourself and others. This is a year for change, but you must be prepared to embrace what is to come.

ROMANCE AND
⚜ FRIENDSHIP ⚜

For most star signs, Saturn is a feared planet, but in your case, it governs excellent astrological directions. This, karmically, makes it your best planet. This doesn't mean that you are not going to have your challenges, as indicated at the outset, but meeting your emotional and marital challenges with a positive attitude will bring immense results to you, leading you to a new level of awareness and a deeper bond of affection between you and your significant other.

If you have been keeping a lid on your feelings and have felt unable to articulate your frustrations, this will continue until the latter part of July when Mars, a not-so-friendly planet for you, makes its entry into your most important marital zone. This will herald the start of a new cycle where you will want to challenge your spouse or partner and get to the bottom of the problems that have been troubling you.

I have often described the combination of Mars and Saturn like a person at the wheel of a car with one foot on the brake and the other on the accelerator. We all know what that means, don't we? A lot of burning rubber, smoke and no movement, which means it's not easy to get to your destination. My advice between July and September is to take a calm and non-reactive approach to what's bothering you and, if necessary, wait it out and discuss them after these transits have passed, no matter how compelled you are to push the issue.

There are some relieving planetary aspects, so I don't want you to think that it is all doom and gloom in the romance department, because it is not. Your ruling planet, Venus, punctuates what seems to be a dire period with some excellent, loving energy, especially in March, April and then again in June, September (when it will be most needed to counteract the Mars and Saturn influence) and then very significantly in late October, when it moves into your zone of marriage. It is at this time that peace is likely to be made.

Relationships on the Rise

I have touched on the general timing of events, but now let's have a look at the important transits of your ruling planets and when they are likely to bring you some romantic benefits.

Leading up to the 17th of January, Venus and Mars produce some angst in your relationships, but this is probably because you are looking for something more, and greener pastures will certainly be on your mind. Redirect these energies into more social activities, especially around the 20th, when the Sun moves into your social sphere.

Because Venus moves to and fro in its retrograde motion, you will experience some of these niggling and unfulfilled passions around the 3rd of March. After the 6th, some exciting new friendships and possibly even romance may emerge from your networking and social connections. A low-key period can be expected between the 6th and 25th of April when Venus passes through the quieter zone of your horoscope and makes a positive aspect to Saturn just before the solar eclipse on the 29th. This may bring you into contact with family members, and there will be a connection to your married life or your romantic involvements. There may also be some disapproval over your choice of partners by members of your family or friends.

The 3rd of May is an excellent date as it indicates the transit of Venus into your Sun sign. This is always welcome because it brings with it a soothing and attractive energy that draws people to you. Don't be too cocky and proud, especially between the 11th and 19th of May, as your ruling planet enters into difficult aspects with Mars, the Sun, Pluto, Uranus and Jupiter, bringing with it a mixed bag of energies that can throw you into emotional confusion.

ROMANTIC SPOTLIGHT

Important transits relating to your love life happen around the 16th of July with the all-important and beneficial Jupiter moving to your zone of love affairs and creativity. Expect an upswing in your romantic life at this time. This is a very positive influence.

If you are looking for something a little wilder or more unusual, then look no farther than the 1st of August when Venus aspects Uranus. You will be taking a walk on the wild side and have a strong need to explore the unknown. Towards the end of the month, after the 27th, you'll need to be on your best behaviour, as diplomacy will win out over antagonism. Talk calmly through your problems.

A much better phase in your relationships takes place after the 30th of September when Venus enters into your zone of marital affairs. Once again, you must not be too compulsive about sorting out any lingering issues. Patience is required, and if you can manage to hang on until the 28th of October, the influence of Neptune on Venus allows you to realise some of your passionate ideals in love.

The end of the year is excellent as Venus moves into the upper part of the horoscope, ensuring a satisfactory romantic close for 2014.

☙ WORK AND MONEY ☙

Harness Your Moneymaking Powers

Making money can be summed up in an equation:

$$m \text{ (\$ money)} = e \text{ (energy)} \times t \text{ (time)} \times l \text{ (love)}$$

If one of these factors is not present—for example, energy or love—you could still make money, but you won't be ideally fulfilled in the process.

It's important to grasp the universal laws of attraction and success when dealing with money. It is also necessary to understand that when you love what you do, you infuse your work with the quality of attention, love and perfection. With these qualities you endow your work with a sort of electromagnetic appeal, a power that draws people to your work and makes them appreciate what you do. This generates a desire for people to use your service, buy your products and respect you for the great work you do. This will elevate you to higher and higher positions because you will be regarded as someone who exercises great diligence and skill in your actions.

One of the highlights of 2014 is the presence of Jupiter in your zone of contracts, communications and daily activities. This planet indicates expansive processes, the ability to grow and achieve success through work, and an ability to negotiate. Bear in mind, however, that Jupiter brings with it some debt or liabilities to Taurus-born individuals, so you need to be prepared to step up to the plate and take some risks this year, but without going overboard.

The other advantage of Jupiter in this sector is that it influences, very powerfully, your zone of business partnerships. For those of you who prefer to go it alone, might I suggest that you consider throwing open the doors and enlist the help of others who will be able to achieve your goals more easily. As the old adage goes, 'Many hands make light work'.

Speaking of partnerships, the presence of Saturn in your zone of business affiliations tells us that you should work with older, more experienced people, even if that may not be 'cool'. Remember when I mentioned the positive influence of Saturn as your supremely good ally? Well, this planet's slow but lucky movement in your zone of partnerships gives us a big hint as to where your best fortunes lie in the next 12 months.

Although you have some secret ideas you wish to develop, you're warned against being rash, impulsive and pushy. This is due to the opposition aspect of Mars and Uranus, which also tells us quite a bit about your attitude to your work environment. Follow the slow and steady energies of Saturn rather than exploding onto the scene with your bright and fresh ideas. You need to rely on your steady Taurean nature to guide you through these exceptionally exciting but also precarious business cycles in 2014.

Legal issues or some bureaucratic entanglements may be part of your fate this year, as shown by the cluster of planets in the ninth zone of legal happenings. Don't get too bogged down in trying to win a fight that may drain your resources and exhaust your mind. Balance the pros and cons, and look at the return on your investment, both creatively and financially. This is the key to coming out on top this year.

Tips for Financial Success

Mercury, Neptune and Jupiter are all important planets for Taurus as they signify personal income and profits if you happen to be independently employed. We can see that Jupiter and Neptune have a more long-term effect, so let's look at how the opposition of Jupiter to Pluto across your work and family axis sets the trend this year.

Power plays seem to be part of your destiny, so you need to be careful with how you balance work and play. Family may be demanding, but employers are too, so divided loyalties will present a problem as the year commences. Finding inner and outer equanimity is essential to finding satisfaction in these key areas of your life.

Because Jupiter moves through your zone of property and family throughout the early part of the year, you will be spending considerable amounts of money beautifying your house and trying to improve your living space, especially after the 2nd week of July. Mercury, Jupiter and the Sun brighten and accentuate your interest in real estate and other fixed assets throughout August. Between late August and September, the connection of Venus to Jupiter is very lucky, so financial upliftment is likely during this period. You may look at investment properties to help you gain the edge financially.

....

RELIEVE THE PRESSURE

When the Sun moves to the sixth zone of debts and health issues, you must be careful not to overwork. This takes place between the 23rd of August and the 22nd of September. My advice is that you should spend some time nourishing yourself and not getting too obsessed with money.

....

Some sudden but fortuitous financial event may occur after the 26th of September with the powerful and positive aspect from Jupiter to Uranus. Expect the unexpected at this time. This also heralds a new cycle of confidence in your business when things can take shape and move forward, but probably from unexpected quarters.

The entry of Venus into your career zone on the 11th of December marks a successful professional cycle when you can anticipate increased cash flow.

Career Moves and Promotions

There are several key dates that you should watch out for, and the first of those is the 1st of February when Venus enters your zone of career. You won't need to make too much of an effort to increase your prospects of a promotion. A small nudge to your employer should be enough, but don't miss this opportunity.

Although the Sun is moving in the zone of workplace activities, it is particularly powerful after the 23rd of August and you must be extremely careful in weighing up your options. You have your eye on the money, but you could overlook what's involved in committing yourself to a new position and it may run you ragged. Make sure you maintain your quality of life if you do go for a new job at this time.

Approaching employers, either within your existing organisation or elsewhere, can bring you success after the 11th of October. Don't take the first position on offer, however, as you may be somewhat impulsive up until the 10th of November.

When Mars transits the upper part of your horoscope on the 11th of November, some excellent opportunities arise and your leadership potential is clearly visible to those who count. On the 11th of December, when Venus enters your zone of career, you may be surprised to find a late opportunity to achieve success and 'ascend the throne'. Better late than never!

When to Avoid Office Politics

One of the inimical planets this year is Mars, so we need to observe when this planet influences your work and career sector.

Mars is adverse in the early part of the year and is particularly challenging around the 19th of January. Work colleagues may not be amenable to your brand of management or ideas. For this reason, you should maintain a low-key approach to sharing your concepts with others.

From the 30th of March, when Venus and Saturn enter into difficult aspect, you need to be careful of those you trust. Someone may inadvertently undermine you and reveal sensitive information that can cause you some grief. This may not be too harrowing at first, but the implications could be long-term. Be careful whom you divulge your secrets to.

There are several important periods, and the first, which commences around the 21st of April and concludes on the solar eclipse of the 29th, shows considerable trouble, disputes, arguments and misunderstandings with co-workers and people in general. Clarify all information being sent via email, and, if possible, get others to sign on the dotted line before agreeing to a course of action.

The other challenging cycles include the 14th to the 25th of June, the 2nd to the 26th of August and the 11th to the 15th of November. During these intervals, you must be alert and clear on other people's motivations. My advice is to stay out of gossip circles and focus on your own personal and professional agenda.

HEALTH, BEAUTY AND
❧ LIFESTYLE ❧

🦋 Venus Calendar for Beauty

Looking great this year won't be too difficult as your ruling planet transits the upper part of your horoscope from as early as the 17th of January. During your ruling planet's transits through your career sector and then after the 6th of March into your social zone, you can expect excellent results up until the 6th or 7th of April. What this means is that your talents, charm and, most importantly, your physical attractiveness, will enhance your personality to bring you first class results in all areas of your life.

Time Out to Refresh

After the 7th of April, you need to take some time out and refresh your outlook and physical being. Issues relating to your skin, complexion and scalp may need to be monitored, and your diet will need to be adequately addressed to keep you looking young and fresh.

When Venus transits your Sun sign after the 3rd of May, many of these niggling physical problems will be replaced with a renewed sense of vigour, adventure and new-found friendships. This is augmented by the Sun's transit of your third house, showing a need for travel, communication and plugging into the social and cultural scene to showcase your talents and good looks.

Venus is favourable on the 25th of August, after the 30th of September, on the 17th of November and finally on the 11th of December when it hits the pinnacle of your horoscope, bringing with it renewed popularity and success.

★★★ Showing off Your Taurus Traits

As I mentioned earlier, you need to keep yourself looking fresh and young. This is not simply about your physical looks, but also about your intellectual openness during 2014. The conjunction of Mercury and Venus after the 14th of January ensures that your communication skills improve. If you are interested in pursuing some sort of study or self-improvement, this is the time to do it. You will be successful, and this will bear out in many other areas of your life.

As Taurus is a fixed sign, you find it hard getting out of your comfort zone. I am pleased to say that a balance of caution and enthusiasm for adventure will make many Taureans break free of their limitations this year.

In the first three months of the year, you have a chance to break free of your 'stuckness', and this can happen when Venus moves into a favourable angle to Saturn. That takes place after the 25th of April. At this time, you mustn't be afraid to show off your sensual, caring and loving nature, which may have been suppressed by too many other things diverting your attention. Of course, Venus, your ruler, is known as the planet of love. Why not display this and show your true nature during these cycles, Taurus.

★★ **Best Ways to Celebrate**

Mercury and Venus, along with the Sun and the Moon, in the sector of travels and higher learning tell us that it is important for you to break free and enjoy other cultures, travelling and even a spiritual expansion. Embracing different environments will make you happy this year. Mercury, your ruler of creativity, love and celebration, is intensely connected to Pluto, the transformative planet. What this means is that some of your enjoyment may come from discovering facets of your personality that you were not aware of. Once this happens, you'll feel joyous and not as limited as you thought.

When Mercury comes to the sign of Pisces in late January and February, you'll rejoice in the company of friends and realise that you have taken them for granted for too long. This realisation can release a lot of joy and happiness, but you mustn't overdo it. People will find it strange that someone who is reluctant to express their feelings is now gushing with joy and love. Again, keep a balanced view and remember that the best relationships are those of give and take.

Because Jupiter occupies the zone of learning and communication, this is one area that will bring you a great deal of happiness. Sharing celebrations with those of similar views and educational leanings will be spotlighted throughout 2014. Making an effort to renew your educational strengths will make you very happy.

KARMA, SPIRITUALITY AND EMOTIONAL BALANCE

It is essential for you to take time out this year, and some of the important dates for doing so occur when your ruling planet moves to the quiet, meditative zone of your horoscope after the 6th of April. Because Uranus will also occupy this part of the zodiac, you may find instant, sudden flashes of insight that may not be easy to articulate but which have a very long-lasting effect on your life, emotions and attitude to life.

HUMANITARIAN INSTINCTS

The twelfth zone of your horoscope has much to do with sharing, charities and humane projects. You may feel prompted to do something out of the ordinary this year, particularly during the phase up to and including the 3rd of May, when you may discover a cause that will open your heart and elevate you spiritually.

Your key spiritual planet is Saturn, and we seem to keep coming back to this throughout 2014. The biggest challenge, but also the most liberating influence, is to work through and understand your role in relationships. Look at others as a mirror to yourself and remember that the difficult or irritating personality traits you see in others only point at some psychological complex within yourself. By doing this, you'll limit your critical attitude and improve your own personality in the process. This will be a major revelation to many Taureans.

The big challenge happens in late July when Mars moves into the same position as Saturn. Biting your tongue and redirecting the torch of awareness on your own shortcomings is difficult, but it will be a key factor in your spiritual evolution, especially over the coming 12 months.

2014

MONTHLY & DAILY PREDICTIONS

INSANITY IS DOING THE SAME
THING, OVER AND OVER AGAIN,
BUT EXPECTING DIFFERENT RESULTS.

Albert Einstein

❦ JANUARY ❧

Monthly Overview

The New Moon in the ninth house indicates the resolution of legal conflicts and the resurgence of interest in some study or higher education. Travel will captivate your attention, and the combination of the Sun and Venus on the 11th of January will also help further your professional activities.

1 You're off to a hectic start today, but be careful not to allow your mind to get too scattered as you deal with work issues. Sidestep arguments.

2 Although a new friendship may begin just now, your cultural or philosophical differences may be too wide a gap to bridge. You don't have to become best friends with everyone.

3 You have a good measure of control just now, and you'll need it as unexpected circumstances push your buttons. Don't react.

4 You are feeling cool, possibly even isolated, at present, but this is a perfect opportunity for you to re-examine yourself and see just where relationships may be falling down. Don't shy away from what needs to be done.

5 You are confused today and likely to absorb the negative energies of others. It's not possible to shut out the world, but don't superimpose or project your negative feelings on others.

6 You have excellent powers of perception and communication at present. Use that to your advantage. You may see things others don't, and this will give you an unfair advantage in your associations.

7 If you have any doubts in a friendship, you'll need to delve deeply to get the truth. Others may be avoiding the important questions you want to ask, but you must persist.

8 Mercury and Venus give you considerable luck and good feelings today. You have an interest in seeking out new topics of interest and possibly even educational programs.

9 Revisiting the past will help you reconnect with your talents and the good things that you have. Maintaining an attitude of gratitude is essential.

10 A promise of bigger and better things may seem lucrative, but it could be invalid at this point in time. Investigate the fine print.

11 You may receive good news that elevates your spirit and makes you feel confident at a time when you have been feeling that you were treading water. Patience will win the day.

12 Mercury enters your career zone, and this gives you an opportunity to request a pay rise or better conditions in your workplace.

13 You can direct your high-powered energy and emotional reactions into constructive work today. Don't be distracted by others who may exhibit envy.

14 You are on the go again and will find yourself busy with too many things. Prioritise what is essential and disregard the rest.

15 Making a journey is fortuitous just now, but you mustn't act in haste. Get all the facts and figures before making a decision.

16 You have a strong, creative flair just now. This can help you, especially if you are looking at redesigning some facet of your home or living space. You are also interested in painting, art and music.

17 A momentary burden seems to be clouding your judgment. Don't make too much of someone else's negativity. Look at the positives today.

18 The news you receive may not satisfy you just now, but don't overreact. The second part is yet to come.

19 Finances require a clever solution today. You have the ability to think outside the square to reduce your debts.

20 You are expansive, generous and possibly wasteful. Don't spend more than you have as you will regret it later.

21 Love affairs may get bogged down in issues of control, and poor communication is the source of this problem. Be as transparent as you expect others to be.

22 You are overworked just now and must not play the role of martyr when others are rallying to help you. Accept a helping hand; it will make a huge difference.

23 Your mind is on love, friendship and other social issues, but work may be pulling you away from that. You need to find a balance between these two areas of your life.

24 Heated discussions need not tear friendships apart. Try to finish any important meeting on a cordial and honourable note.

25 Your thinking is slow and your memory may be poor, so don't enter into battle without having all the facts. This is a good way to avoid embarrassment.

26 You are out of step with cultural trends, so if you are invited to an engagement that is a little different, you may need to keep a very open mind to enjoy it.

27 Children may be devious, especially if you are a parent. You need to think like a deceptive person to understand the true nature of an issue today.

28 Legal matters may bother you. There are times when you need to enlist the help of professionals. It may cost you a little money, but it will give you peace of mind.

29 You are on edge just now, but what are you worried about? Perhaps nothing; it may be just a vague feeling of uneasiness. Distract yourself with something that is fun.

30 Bring a touch of emotion to your work; a clinical approach often leaves others high and dry. Show your human face to move forward professionally.

31 Professional communications are occupying your mind. This is also an excellent time to catch up on work that has piled up on your in-tray. You will be relieved when you clear the decks.

☆ FEBRUARY ☆

👤 *Monthly Overview*

Socialising with others and meeting new people may be triggered by your strong ideals and desire. However, be careful not to put others on a pedestal, especially between the 3rd and the 8th of the month. Workplace clashes may occur this month, but if you are diplomatic in your approach you can sidestep some of these issues.

1 Others may not understand your ideas today. As the old saying goes, 'Don't throw pearls before swine'. Seek out those who are progressive enough to appreciate your creativity.

2 Your high standards may spill over into your social friendships, which is why others may not be meeting your expectations. Don't get mad about it—get a new circle of friends.

3 Meditation, stillness and introversion are essential to recharge your batteries. Now is one of those times.

4 Just as you settle into a bit of 'me' time, a spanner is thrown into the works. You may need to disrupt your quiet lifestyle to attend to a pressing problem.

5 You have a strong sense of self-awareness at the moment, which means that you can eradicate habits or vices that are holding you back in life. In other words, reiterate your New Years' resolution, if you had one. If not, it is never too late to turn over a new leaf.

6 Remember, there is no progress without deviation, so don't be afraid to try something outside the square. You'll discover something fascinating.

7 By listening more carefully you'll draw others nearer to you. The art of listening is important for developing and deepening your relationships today.

8 Your imagination is running wild, and if you don't restrain your fantasies, you could run into difficulties, especially where relationships are concerned. If you have a niggling doubt, ask the other person about it.

9 You want to go to an impromptu outing but will find yourself out of sorts. Regret may linger throughout the event.

10 Speculation is not advised at the moment, but you may still want to take a punt. This is not a problem as long as you are judicious with the amount of money you spend.

11 Contracts may need to be ratified under this transit. Don't be afraid to challenge certain points, especially if they disadvantage you.

12 A heavy responsibility may weigh on you, but you don't have the support of others. Courage and resilience are needed.

13 Communication from your spouse or partner is vague or, at worst, deceptive. Trust your intuition to get to the root cause.

14 You can learn something from those you least expect, and the information will excite you. By keeping an open mind you will develop your inner awareness.

15 Your energy is very strong, but so is your desire to get things done quickly. If you push others beyond their limits, you will make enemies.

16 It is not an all-or-nothing situation, even though you think it is. Continue to communicate your feelings and needs and you will be surprised at how much others are prepared to compromise.

17 You can manifest anything you want; it is only your self-doubt holding you back. Study the laws of power and karma and implement these in your life to gain what you desire.

18 A reward you have been waiting for may suddenly arrive, but don't be surprised if it is less than you expected. Be thankful for small graces.

19 You will have a great time within your social circle, but you must concede and go along with others' wishes. If this is part of give-and-take in the larger scheme of things, all will be well. Otherwise, you will have to force someone's hand to get your way.

20 You have little time today and a load of work that you are falling behind on. The best thing you can do is systematise your work approach.

21 You can renew an old friendship, but don't be surprised if there is a considerable gap in the way you perceive things now.

22 Knowledge is power, but only when the knowledge you gain is of use to you. Being a bookworm simply to retain facts and figures is a useless exercise.

23 You need to shake up some friendship or long-term relationship today to move into a new cycle with that person. Initially there will be fear, but later they will thank you for kicking them up the proverbial behind.

24 If you have to make a decision that is not popular, it will take a great deal of courage. You will be torn between two factions or sets of ideas. Adhere to your truth today.

25 You need to re-evaluate your direction, particularly if you have been listening to too many outsiders. Only you know what's best for you, but you need to dig deep to find that today.

26 If you feel erratic and scattered in your responses to others, it is best to postpone any important discussions. Regroup your energies and reschedule.

27 You could misplace your affections today by trying to see the best in others to justify your position. On the question of material goods, keep a tight rein on your money and possessions, and don't loan things to anyone today.

28 You may find it difficult to resolve some issue at work, especially if the solutions are beyond your scope of expertise. Don't waste too much time on this problem. Put it to the side and complete your other tasks first.

☙ MARCH ☙

Monthly Overview

This can be a successful month for you, but impulse, passion and a reckless nature may undo much of the good that destiny has in store for you. Professional accolades and promotions are indicated, as are new friendships, especially after the 6th of March. In the last week of the month, your affection for someone you love or felt close to may cool off, but this is only temporary.

1   You are feeling confident today, but a stray comment may undermine that if you allow it to. Keep the compass pointing north and don't allow others to tear you down.

2   You may be dissatisfied with the way your spouse or partner is handling money. This is more pertinent if you are in a business relationship with someone and their fiscal prudence is lacking. Renegotiation is necessary.

3   You will get assistance to remove blocks within your mental, emotional or spiritual life today, but once assistance is given, will you act on it?

4 You may not want to hear some spiritual truth at present, but it can transform your life if your ego is held in check. Others may help you now.

5 You have a desire to seek out and explore unresolved desires. Balance your karmic appetites with tasteful behaviour today.

6 As Venus transits your tenth house, your popularity will grow, as will your professional success. Combine the two and a little magic can happen today.

7 Don't be shy in coming forward, especially if you are single and see someone attractive. The rules of the game have changed: if you are a girl, it is quite okay to ask a guy out on a date.

8 Miscommunications can land you in trouble at present. Check everything you write before sending it via email.

9 You may be asked to offer more than you are prepared to give, so weigh up the positives as well as the negatives. Finding a happy medium will be your task today.

10 You're impatient with others who can't see your point of view. Your communication is also faster and more dynamic, so try not to hang out with boring people.

11 Unusual relationships may develop—and quickly.
Slow the pace, even if it seems like a knight in shining
armour or a princess has come to save you from your
routine existence.

12 You need to take the right course of action to gain the
respect and admiration of others in your workplace
today. Stand by your decisions and creative impulses,
even if others ridicule you.

13 Keep things simple now, especially in your
communications. Saying too much will give things away.
Maintaining an air of mystery will give you the edge.

14 If you feel uncomfortable discussing some private issues,
it might be better to approach someone who is not as
close if you want impartial advice.

15 You have some good karma coming now, but if you are
oblivious to the signals, you may miss the boat. Look out
for cues that fortuitous events are about to happen.

16 You are more concerned with your own self-
understanding and personal affairs than socialising or
being with others. In fact, if someone calls on you today,
it could simply be an irritation.

17 Health issues, albeit niggling small ones, may reduce the enjoyment of your day. Don't allow any physical discomfort to go unchecked. Your yearly medical may be due.

18 Some impulses are transient and you mustn't act on them immediately. Jot down what you want, sleep on it and see whether the urges are still strong tomorrow.

19 Someone may deliberately try to undermine you at present, and how you react or don't react will determine the outcome. You may have to do some 'posturing' to make this person back down.

20 A favourable opportunity may arise at work. Are you game enough to take it? If you become complacent, it may pass you by. Jump at it.

21 You need to circulate professionally. If you have been stuck in a rut, you may need to reconnect with people who are the mainstay of your business and who can help it grow.

22 There may be disagreements over style when it comes to purchasing furniture or other household items. Once again, a compromise may be necessary to keep everyone happy.

23 Dealing with shared finances is always touch-and-go. You need a mediator such as an accountant, attorney or someone in the know to balance differing views on these matters.

24 Mercury enters your eleventh zone of profitability in the company of Neptune. Don't be afraid to live your dreams and manifest your vision for financial security.

25 You may be looking at medical alternatives such as herbs or other New Age practices to help sort out your physical and psychological wellbeing. Be balanced in your views and make sure you are not dealing with quacks.

26 You are losing a lot of time, so rearrange your schedule and redefine the nature of your business relationships. Prioritise the people who will be of benefit to you.

27 You need to cut back on expenses, and you may realise that budgeting, or rather lack of budgeting, is the cause of escalating expenses in your life. Tighten your belt.

28 Financial issues continue to be on the top of your agenda. Simplification is the key to coming through this with a positive outcome.

29 Don't be too serious today as it will provoke negative responses. A little humour will go a long way.

30 Friends may be warring and it is time for you to step in and act as a mediator or judge. This will defuse some of the negative energy within your peer group.

31 Passion is on the rise, but because Venus and Mars affect your workplace, this may not be a good idea. Keep work relationships professional.

APRIL

Monthly Overview

The Sun is powerful this month, even though it is in the hidden part of your horoscope. Take pleasure in your own company and don't feel coerced into being with others if you don't want to. Despite this, you will have ample opportunity to engage others and enjoy dinners, outings and other one-on-one social endeavours throughout the month. Around the 9th, be careful of your health and avoid speed at any cost.

1 By all means share your ideas with friends, but don't be drawn into contentious issues just now. You need to keep the peace rather than proving you are right.

2 You have strong intuition, which means that you don't need to rely on others to tell you where your relationships are going today. Trust your instinct if you feel that all is not well with someone.

3 Don't make out that you know more than you do. Humility is your key word today, and besides, you can learn more when you listen.

4   You're feeling as if time is slipping away from you. With increased deadlines, you may be tempted to escape, but if you do so, you will only create a snowball effect. Do today's tasks immediately.

5   Venus and Jupiter continue to provide a great deal of luck, especially in your professional activities. You don't need to make too much effort. By the same token, don't become too big-headed.

6   You may think you are helping others, but instead you are becoming a martyr. Analyse those who are deserving and those who aren't.

7   It is difficult meeting people who have similar ideals, but it may happen through a chance encounter. A meeting of minds is likely.

8   You don't have to justify your choice of friends to others. If someone is questioning you, it may be a case of jealousy.

9   You need to discover your inner child if you want to get through the day. Avoid a serious state of mind, if at all possible. Remain playful.

10 You may do things on a whim today, but that is okay as long as it doesn't cost money. Your imagination is not in sync with the practical reality of things.

11 You have your heart set on something at present, but others may try to dissuade you from carrying out your plans. You will need to weigh up the pros and cons.

12 You feel a great sense of emotional harmony, but those around you don't. Hold on to your own good feelings and don't be dragged down by those around you.

13 For some reason you feel embarrassed about asking someone for help. There is no shame in this, and by doing so you'll find yourself reducing the tasks on your agenda today.

14 You need to reconnect with a sibling or neighbour you have lost contact with. If the past has been tumultuous, you must start again with a fresh perspective.

15 Friends may dare you or ask you to do something that is out of character. Yes, there is thrill value, but will you feel right about doing it?

16 A special effort will have to be made to connect more deeply with your lover. You may be holding on to a grudge or recollecting negative experiences. Put that aside to elevate the relationship.

17 Solving a stubborn problem requires listening to another person's point of view today. Use empathy as a way of resolving these issues.

18 You may think that something is stolen or lost, but it is just an oversight on your part. Don't think about it too much as it will turn up without much effort on your part.

19 A friend in need may demand time today. Be judicious about how you do this as you don't want to create problems for yourself by overlooking your responsibilities.

20 Self-forgiveness is the key today, and you need to let go of elements in your personality that you don't like. Removing negative thinking will have a tonifying effect on your life.

21 You have skills you aren't employing at work, so you need to use them outside your usual nine-to-five job. Rise above your feelings of inadequacy and tiredness.

22 Societal events may bother you. This could relate to the news or some word on the grapevine. Remember, you must start with your own circle of influence to positively impact the world.

23 You may receive good news that a pay rise or additional cash may be on its way. This is good karma.

24 You are receiving mixed messages from someone you love. Until you clarify what's on their mind, don't be too generous with your time.

25 You need to show some anger to get someone to move in the direction you want. Procrastination will perpetuate the problem.

26 You need to create a line in the sand, otherwise people will take advantage of you. The ball is in your court, and if you continue to be victimised, you have only yourself to blame.

27 An unexpected trip or outing will result in excessive effort for little gain or satisfaction. Think twice before going out today.

28 The best predictor of future behaviour is the past. This goes for yourself and others. Study your history before venturing into some new direction.

29 Don't be too frivolous with friends as they may not take you seriously. To get your point across, take a slower, more measured approach.

30 Your mind is scheming to find ways of increasing income and finding greater creative satisfaction, which is good. Mercury, however, makes you hasty and lacking in clear planning.

✤ MAY ✤

👔 *Monthly Overview*

Your personal strength and attractiveness reaches a peak around the 3rd. Use your power of persuasion wisely. Passions are strong around the 11th, but up until the 20th you should judge others with a clear and calculating mind. Don't wear your heart on your sleeve. Travels take place after the 21st.

1   Success has a great deal to do with your thinking processes. You need to act wealthy if you want to attract wealth.

2   If you are feeling intellectually inferior, you need to do something about it. Expanding your understanding of different subjects is imperative at present. You'll regain any lost confidence.

3   Don't allow envy to bring down your current relationships. You may look at others and wish that you had what they have. Be satisfied with what you've got.

4   You are frustrated because you will receive news about someone that is not clear. You'll need to be patient to get the full picture.

5   Communications with close members of your family are harmonious at present. A greater flow of information ensures domestic satisfaction.

6   You find it hard to understand how people can spend so much money on useless things. You need to curb your urge to express judgment today.

7   You need to be more active to improve your physical wellbeing. This will impact positively on your mind and emotions.

8   Mercury will increase your business turnover and trigger ideas for generating cash. You may be discouraged to learn that someone you trust doesn't support some of your ideas.

9   Weigh up how much you are going to spend on a fight. Bad outcomes are not going to work in your favour right now.

10   Finding a genuine mentor is difficult. If you meet someone who has spiritual insights, this is a good time to allocate quality time with them.

11 The spark of life doesn't burn so brightly today. Those you work with could be part of the problem.

12 You don't need to argue about money, but you need to assert your position to gain control, especially within the family. Power plays are likely.

13 You are giving more consideration to the path you are on at present. If it is not working for you, reappraise where you would like to be.

14 You need to embellish the truth if you want to spend more money from the family kitty. You may also need to sweeten the news by buying a small gift for those who are trying to wrest control from you.

15 You are thinking about someone, and your mind is like a broken record. Single Taureans may be falling in love at this time.

16 Don't put others on a pedestal. They may fall harder than you expect when you realise they are only human. Accept that people have human frailties.

17 A love affair may sour, but you'll realise very quickly that the differences were too great to reconcile. Relax.

18 Your current relationship may take an unexpected turn, but if you follow through with it, a positive outcome is likely. You need to work closely with your mate to overcome the negativity associated with these sorts of events.

19 There could be a clash of wills if you allow yourself to be provoked by someone with an equally strong will. Try to play the game by being gracious and more humble.

20 Worry rarely solves any problems. Substitute your anxiety with a practical plan of attack.

21 You need friends just now, and any sort of isolation will make you feel grumpy. Seek out people who have similar interests today.

22 You have a desire to share your success with others, but if someone is not doing so well, they will see this as an insult, even if it is not intended. Hide your good fortune for the time being.

23 You are inclined to conserve rather than spend or invest in speculative ventures. This is a good route for you to take today.

24 Dreams and wished-for luxuries can be yours if you are brave enough to believe you deserve them! Stand up and stake your claim.

25 Ethical issues may bother you, or the way someone else is conducting themselves may be at odds with your principles. All you need to do is adhere to your own standards.

26 Your imagination is in overdrive, and you feel like making exciting plans with friends. Enjoy the burst of intellectual energy. You will be participating in some interesting conversations today.

27 You can resurrect an old idea that may have been ahead of its time. Try to use your existing network of friends and work colleagues to see how you can develop it.

28 If you are submerging your hurt feelings, it will only cause more grief in your relationship. Someone may not want to hear what is going on in your heart. In this case, you need an alternative outlet—quickly.

29 It's good to question other people's beliefs and viewpoints. If you press too hard, however, you may find yourself in a clash of belief systems. Tread carefully.

30 Friendly competitiveness may turn into something more serious, so manage the situation with humour. On the other hand, you may have to concede defeat to keep the peace.

31 People aren't going to change because you expect them to. Forcing their hand won't work either. Leading by example is the best way.

JUNE

Monthly Overview

Finances are on the up-and-up, and work is more satisfying. There may be an intense period of focus between the 9th and the 13th when you need to re-examine your finances and expenditure. Some fortuitous contractual arrangement between the 23rd and the 29th can help you achieve some of your ambitions.

---

1 You are impatient to get things done today, but an oversight is likely if you try to rush across the finish line. A more measured approach is advisable due to the aspect of the Moon and Uranus.

---

2 You are aggressive about money today, and your desires and reasoning are playing second fiddle to your emotions. If you have had financial problems, don't lash out. Cooperation is needed.

---

3 You may want peace of mind, but problems may pile up and threaten your equanimity. The Moon and Saturn are responsible.

---

4 You are not feeling too connected to others right now. Don't try to pretend you are enjoying the conversation. It's best to bow out gracefully.

5 Friends and family want privileges and concessions, and you're prone to giving it to them without proper scrutiny. You need a new approach today.

6 Progress doesn't happen overnight, and you need to understand that there are many components to achieving your goals. Have a backup plan.

7 You are intellectually competitive at the moment, but no one is giving you enough of a challenge. You need to seek greener pastures for your mind.

8 Don't be too ostentatious in the way you present yourself. Your self-image could be more important than you think, and others will judge you harshly.

9 You are not receiving what you believe is fair compensation for your efforts in love. You don't feel respected, but talking is not the way to get results. Actions speak louder than words.

10 You mustn't compare yourself to others because everyone's talents are unique. Look at your abilities and try to develop them rather than playing the comparison game.

11 You have to lift someone else's spirits today, and this may not be easy. It may seem like a daunting task, but it will help you develop creative skills in dealing with others.

12 You're worried about money, but overcoming financial issues is a better approach. You need a complete shift in the way you manage money right now.

13 You may have some unusual dreams about future events. This may scare you, but being forewarned means that you are forearmed.

14 Your life may become humdrum unless you dig deeper and find meaning in the little things. Transform everything you do into a divine action.

15 If you feel a strong conviction about something today, why are you trying to convince everyone else? The reason could be insecurity.

16 You might be upset by someone who raises inappropriate issues at the wrong time. You need to take control and postpone these discussions.

17 If you have agreed to help too many people, your schedule is going to be pushed to the limit. Time your appointments, particularly the favours you are doing for others.

18 Mercury endows you with the gift of the gab today, but use this power wisely; don't waste it on idle gossip.

19 Expenditure related to work may leave you feeling angry, but begrudging it is the wrong approach. Look at it as a way of investing in future growth.

20 You mustn't be agreeable and forfeit your own opinions to be popular. Speak your truth and respect will be forthcoming.

21 You may think you are listening carefully, but you will be surprised when you realise how much you missed. Have you thought of taking a recorder to important meetings to tape what is being said?

22 Getting to the bottom of a problem today requires silence, not words. If you can sit still, the unconscious mind will reveal a lot more than you anticipated.

23 There is excitement in the air, but also an element of apprehension. If this has to do with meeting someone new, simply relax and go with the flow.

24 Lucky Venus has entered your financial zone, which means that economic concerns should start to lift now.

25 You may receive news of an engagement or a party, but you won't be able to attend. Today is a day of other priorities.

26 You want to spend lavishly today, so try to purchase items that will retain some value or be seen as an investment. This way you won't be spending money; you'll be earning it.

27 You have to reassess your abilities and skills in the light of prevailing trends around you. Try to be unbiased and honest in your self-appraisal.

28 If you are dealing with someone else's dishonesty or negative personality traits, you will be tested. You need to change the rules of the game to come out on top.

29 Home affairs overlap wonderfully with creative pursuits. Engage other family members in some of your ideals and plans.

30 Re-evaluating a creative idea or financial position doesn't mean you have to throw the baby out with the bath water. Use the work and time you have invested and build upon it.

☆ JULY ☆

👤 *Monthly Overview*

Your willpower is obstructed around the 3rd, but you mustn't chew on this issue like a dog with a bone. Redirect your energies and attention to something more productive. You feel scattered up until the 13th, after which your affections, communication and romantic affairs will stabilise. Some lucky meeting may develop into a relationship after the 16th. Love affairs continue to blossom until the end of the month, but be careful of health issues after the 26th.

---

1 It's not *what* you say but *how* you say it that will make the difference. If you are in command, others may resent this. Be gentle with how you dish out your directives.

---

2 Mercury is very powerful at present, and an idea you had been struggling with will become crystal clear. This has to do with money.

---

3 Just when you thought a relationship was back on track, it has derailed again. You will have to keep working on this one. Isn't that the name of the game with all relationships?

---

4   Forgiveness is the key word right now, but if your memory is hanging on to past hurts, this is not going to be easy.

5   If you are thinking too much about what you're earning, you might not be in the right line of work. You may have to think deeply about alternatives today.

6   You are endowed with lots of energy as the Moon and Mars connect in your zone of work. This could also mean patching up an old friendship that has gone bad.

7   If your travel plans have gone awry, it could be because you were too optimistic and didn't account for unforseen costs. Go back and sharpen your pencil.

8   Someone has done you a favour, but now you've discovered that there are strings attached. There is no easy way to get around this other than to bite the bullet and remember for next time.

9   You will have to deal patiently with a stupid relative who is not as savvy as you. Don't let your arrogance overtake you. There may be something you can learn from the experience.

10 You could become fascinated by a topic that previously left you cold. It may overlap into other areas you have an interest in. Keep the doors of exploration open.

11 Being a leader can cause you to puff out your chest, but don't forget that you have additional responsibilities that go along with it. Achievement comes with sacrifice.

12 You are weighing up your options today, and you will realise that an ethical benefit far outweighs a material one. This is the path to inner happiness.

13 A reunion is a great way to bring old work colleagues back together, at least for a short time. It is also a great way for you to learn how others are tackling the same problems.

14 Don't assume a course of action when you haven't been given clear directions. Remember, if you assume something, it makes an ass out of you and me.

15 The Moon enters your zone of self-fulfilment and profits, which means that a promotion is likely during this phase. Money is high on your agenda, but so are social interactions. Money and friends will be satisfying.

16 You are astrally absorptive today. This means that you should be careful about the people you hang out with. You'll absorb positive and negative emotions from whomever you come into contact.

17 You can make more money right now, but you have a tendency to spend it before you earn it. Measured approaches are best, and don't allow ostentation to dictate your spending habits.

18 You will need to keep someone at arm's length today, especially if you know that they have been taking you for a ride. Being conspicuously absent for a while will send the right message.

19 Mercury and Neptune will help you make gains by not necessarily speaking the whole truth today. This isn't lying, just convenient omission.

20 You may be harsh in your discipline, but remember that what goes around comes around. Treat others as you would like to be treated yourself.

21 Stationary Saturn is a heavy task master for married people today. Some vital lesson about love and commitment may be emerging.

22 You are in two minds about what to do financially. To spend, or not spend, that is the question. But you may not have to make a decision today. Sleep on it.

23 Too many family members require your attention today. Get back to an orderly system of addressing them one by one.

24 If you have hit mid-life and believe that there is no way you can achieve your dreams, put that thought aside once and for all. Remember, Michelangelo was in his 60s when he painted the Sistine Chapel.

25 You may think you can do more than you can today. As a result, you will bite off more than you can chew. Step back and think again.

26 Contentious Mars enters your zone of marriage and relationships today. Try not to take the bait if someone is in an argumentative mood.

27 If you have exercised self-control for a day or so, Mars will prod you again and you may not be able to hold back. Don't say anything you will regret.

28 Gambling is okay as long as you don't throw away good money on a whim or advice from those who don't know any better. Research your investments before venturing forth to gamble.

29 Little fish are sweet, which means that even the smallest successes can compound over time to create a larger success. Slow and steady wins the race.

30 You have a genuine need to help someone today, but not for any particular reason. This is your compassionate side coming out.

31 Don't trust everyone you meet. Check for alternative motives before giving your heart away.

AUGUST

Monthly Overview

Your desire is strong between the 1st and the 7th. Learn to recognise when enough is enough and someone is taking advantage of you. Heavy responsibilities can be expected between the 10th and the 23rd. This may impact on your health again, so increase your vitamin intake and get adequate rest. Frustrations around the 26th may cause you to say and do things that you will regret later.

1 You want to spread your wings today, but workplace responsibilities prohibit it. Moreover, your mind can't focus because you're worried about someone on the home front.

2 You're nitpicking and focusing on an error you made. Get over it! We all make mistakes; learn from them.

3 Don't be hasty in throwing out something you think is old or of no use anymore. Some items may increase in value over time.

4 The hard aspect of the Moon to the Sun and Saturn is not great today, and it could slow you down. If that's the case, enjoy the ride at a lesser speed.

5 You want more sensuality from your relationships. There is no point wishing for something. Be proactive rather than reactive.

6 Someone will make you a business offer, but you may have to rely on feeling rather than rational deduction. You don't have to give them an answer on the spot.

7 Your willpower is obstructed at present. Water, however, assumes any shape and overcomes even the biggest obstructions. Be like water today.

8 Your thinking is out of sync with your peer group or family. You need to have the courage to be an individual and move along your own lines.

9 Take a short break if work or people are overcrowding you. You'll come back refreshed and with new insights.

10 It is important to ask for people's opinions, even if it comes in the form of criticism. If this is the case, you should be pleased that you can now improve certain aspects of your personality.

11 You don't feel as if the people around you have the same level of enthusiasm. This can be very draining. Are you able to take a short holiday until everyone snaps out of it? Good idea!

12 An older female, perhaps your mother, may be feeling despondent or unwell. You will need to be there for her.

13 The word 'no' is one of the most powerful in the English language. Have you learnt how to say it? It is important today as people are demanding their pound of flesh from you.

14 You're daydreaming and unable to focus on the task at hand. You may not like what you are doing. You need to re-engage with your work.

15 A shopping spree is necessary as someone's birthday or anniversary is looming on the horizon. You may be tempted to buy a gift certificate, but personalise the occasion by making a greater effort.

16 If you and someone else are having similar problems, it may be useful to pool your mental and emotional resources to come up with a solution.

17 You're thinking about love, but you may be nostalgically reminiscing about your youth and what used to be. Come back to the present and look forward to the future.

18 Don't get too comfortable in any relationship or friendship. Today maybe one of those days when you need to throw a spanner in the works to keep the relationship alive.

19 Lucky Venus and Jupiter combine in your zone of domestic and family matters. There should be some sort of good news or cause for enjoyment.

20 You can't allow others to keep annoying you and disrupting your flow, especially at work. It is time to put up the 'do not disturb' sign.

21 Someone may accuse you of having said or done something you can't recall. You need to get them to document this or prove it in writing.

22 Step outside the square today and do things on your own terms. You may be fearful that others will point the finger of blame at you, but the results will speak for themselves.

23 Delving into the mysteries of death, reincarnation and other topics may scare you. But this line of enquiry may be opened up by someone and you'll be fascinated by where it can take you.

24 If you are feeling unappreciated, you may need to bring awareness of your virtues and talents to others. You mustn't feel any shame in doing this.

25 Transformative forces abound, and with the Moon, Venus and the Sun impacting upon your mind, you're ready for change.

26 Don't argue if someone comments on your fashion or makeup today. Go along with it and experiment with alternatives.

27 Sometimes you need to accept that others won't go along with you or support you. Mars and Saturn will produce frustrating energies, but you mustn't become too embroiled in these negative forces.

28 You're probably wondering whether or not your relationship standards are high enough today. You're the one setting those trends, and the partner you choose will reflect your state of mind and social or spiritual calibre.

29 You're passionate about a topic at the moment, and you may be equally passionate in the bedroom. You mustn't use brute force to get your way. Charm will work like magic.

30 Upbeat conversations characterise the transits today. You'll enjoy reaching for the stars with friends, both mentally and creatively. Expand your horizons.

31 You'll be feeling diplomatic at the moment. Don't rush into anything unless there are safeguards built into it. You need to make a decision, even if someone else is urging you to do otherwise.

✲ SEPTEMBER ✲

🔲 *Monthly Overview*

Your energies return to a state of balance from the 3rd, and you are able to refocus your attention on work matters around the 4th, 6th and 14th. Don't believe everything a medical practitioner tells you after the 22nd. Trust your intuition, and don't take pharmaceuticals that may adversely affect you and make your health problems worse. A resurgence of love occurs after the 23rd, and there will be some lovely surprises from your partner around the 30th.

1 You have a competitor, but you need to learn how to manage him/her. Having an all-out stoush is not the way. Learn the art of diplomacy.

2 You mustn't share your supply of funds and power until you have build up an adequate supply. Consolidate your position first.

3 Reorganising your work environment may cost you money and time. Even if you can ill-afford it now, the benefits will far outweigh the costs.

4   You want to do things in a really big way today. Partnering up with someone else will share the burden of costs and energy.

5   Being a creature of habit, you need to step out and try different things and achieve better results. Today is a day of difference.

6   Your creative impulse is strong as Venus moves through your zone of entertainment, pleasure and creativity. Now is the time to take up a new creative interest.

7   Your emotions are out of sync with your will. What you want to do is not supported by your emotions. Head and heart must be in tune.

8   The 80/20 rule is important today. In other words, if you are putting 80 per cent of your efforts into something that is only giving you a 20 per cent return, you need to reverse the equation.

9   Your investigative mind will be called on to research something unusual. In the process, you will uncover additional information that will be helpful in other areas of your life.

10 Is the cup half full or half empty today? Focusing on what you don't have is only going to make things worse.

11 Deep, unconscious urges dominate your mental landscape today. Rather than resisting them, study where they take you within yourself.

12 Let your money work for you; the old adage of working smart is as important as working hard.

13 You are doing a disproportionate amount of work today and need to call someone out on this. Although they will retaliate, they know you are right.

14 Disputes over money are looming as Mars enters your eighth house. Someone could be using money as a form of leverage or punishment.

15 You're probably too intense about love, which will give someone else the edge over you. Pull back a little and it will make you more desirable.

16 You have excellent opportunities to forge a new business deal right now, but you need to do this in stages. Someone whose support you need may take a little longer to come around.

17 You'll feel as if you're the lone voice in the crowd today. Originality is your key word, so don't budge.

MONTHLY PREDICTIONS

18 Because Venus and the Sun make you more desirable, others are more likely to accept your viewpoint and respect you. Bask in the sunshine of love.

19 You can lead a horse to water but you can't make it drink. Offer advice, by all means, but don't expect someone to take it.

20 Mental strength is a component of courage. You may be afraid of losing friends and will compromise your values. You mustn't do this.

21 You're feeling down today, not because of anything you have done, but because you could be empathising with someone, perhaps a child who is undergoing some difficulties. Let them know you are there if they need you.

22 Reconsider your diet and how it may be affecting your physical wellbeing and emotions. You may be experiencing an allergy or reaction to different foods or chemicals.

23 The past is full of problems, and this is the stuff that fertiliser is made of. A clever gardener uses his manure to grow beautiful flowers. Likewise, grow from your painful experiences.

24 Give and take is your key phrase at present, and although you feel as though you've given way too much, you need to set the example today by conceding just a little bit more.

25 You're ready for some lunar illumination as Jupiter and Uranus influence your spiritual sectors. Plug into alternative views of life.

26 Someone may put the hard word on you to borrow money or loan some of your possessions. This is not advisable.

27 Concede your mistake today, and you will create fertile ground for growth and bonding in your relationships.

28 Unwanted attention by someone may create discomfort or even embarrassment for you. You need to be creative when dealing with this.

29 Exploring new avenues of intimacy and lovemaking may be uncomfortable at first, but they can be gateways to deeper emotional and spiritual understanding.

30 There may be a lull in your relationships as Venus enters a difficult zone of your horoscope. Accept that this is part of the cycle of life. Don't make too much of it.

OCTOBER

Monthly Overview

Power plays are likely around the 4th, but with some clever sidestepping, you can gain control of unruly people between the 5th and the 8th, especially if you are an employer or team leader. The period between the 9th and the 25th may make you feel out of step with your peers. Don't feel as if you have to toe the line. Maintain your individuality this month. Some solution to a financial problem can take place from the 28th.

1 The solution to a niggling problem may come from an unexpected area or person. Just call it one of life's bonuses.

2 Your true home is not bricks and mortar, Taurus; it is where your heart is. Understand this when considering a move.

3 You are worried about cash flow right now, but you may have forgotten some additional resources, such as tax refund cheques and so on. Remain optimistic that you can and will overcome your financial concerns.

4 You have more support than you think, and if you are planning a lifestyle change, share these ideas with the ones you love. They will be more than willing to help you achieve your goals.

5 You could come into contact with a younger person who knocks your socks off. Ladies, don't be afraid to explore relationships that are unconventional.

6 You're ready for change now, and a friend may be the catalyst for doing so. Sharing some creative pursuit will also accelerate this process.

7 There may be moments of social awkwardness, and you are not feeling completely accepted. Don't run away. Hold your ground and you will be accepted in time.

8 The trick to being spontaneous is not allowing your mind to filter your feelings. This is a challenge for Taurus, but brilliant results can be expected if you do this.

9 Some past hurt or suppressed experience can be resolved under the eclipse today. Meditate and eliminate.

10 You are scurrying about, which is due to Mercury's influence. Don't rush meetings or discussions. Cutting corners will simply mean redoing the job.

11 You need to create a challenge today, otherwise boredom will set in. Don't sweep unfinished business under the rug.

12 Unrelated incidents, much like a puzzle, can be pieced together now to create a clearer picture of events. Use this to your advantage.

13 The Moon and Venus indicate the love of someone at work or a love of work itself. In any case, it should be a satisfying day.

14 You'll get serious now and curtail your expenses. You also realise that your employees may not be up to the standard that you require. Change this.

15 Are you receiving cryptic messages from someone, or is it all in your imagination? Why keep guessing when you can come straight out and ask the question.

16 Remember, once a word leaves your mouth, you can't take it back. Although you may find someone disagreeable, your challenge is to remain soft-spoken and courteous.

17 You can meet an enemy on their own terms today and patch up a long-standing problem. This individual has information that can fulfil some of your professional requirements.

18 Reserve some money, even if you feel confident you have enough. An unexpected expense could take you by surprise.

19 Spiritual celebration should be a cultural or civil duty. You'll gain more than you expect through this transit.

20 If you've been in an abusive relationship, you can eliminate it from your life right now. Your key word today it transformation. But be warned, this is not a simple task.

21 You need to show your compassion today by helping others who are disadvantaged. You will feel a sense of satisfaction if you act as a catalyst for good.

22 You're juggling too many commitments, and at some point you'll drop the ball. Reappraise your priorities today.

23 Posture is part of your problem at the moment. There are indications that you may be suffering from lower back pain. Monitor the height of your computer screen and chair.

24 You have to be a taskmaster today and exert your power over someone, even if that makes you feel uncomfortable. They will appreciate your concern.

25 Someone else's radical views will make you think more deeply about a topic that has wider ramifications.

26 If someone owes you money, you will feel embarrassed about persistently asking them for it. You need to have some sort of ultimatum up your sleeve.

27 Excellent transits give you a new lease of life, which can also create a resurgence of love for someone, particularly if your feelings had waned recently.

28 Reaffirm the commitment to your life choices. Doing this can give you more energy and inspire you—and others—further.

29 Having a wild imagination is fine, but if what's floating through your mind is completely impractical, you need to eliminate the elements that have no bearing on your life.

30 If you're in a business relationship, you may have to decide whether your partner has the same goals as you. If they don't, you could get distracted and consider other opportunities.

31 Your determined mind may be thrown off course by needy people in your professional sphere. Put out these bushfires to get back on track.

❧ NOVEMBER ❧

Monthly Overview

Exciting but challenging workplace developments can create confusion. Stick to your guns and push for that coveted position up to the 13th. Relationships may sour at this time, but don't complicate things; allow your partner space to work through their problems. Take some time out and travel, if you can, around the 17th. You will enjoy your time away up until the 21st. A previous meeting may have floundered only to be resuscitated again after the 27th. Don't trust your intuition too much after the 28th. Base your judgments on observation, not just feeling.

1 Reconsider your educational qualifications during this phase. You don't necessarily have to go back to full-time study. Learning a new skill, even via correspondence, will help.

2 You admire someone now, possibly a friend, but don't forget that they are also human, and that you, too, have unique traits that make you the individual you are.

3 You have a lot more control over your feelings today as the Moon and Saturn provide you with a clear vision and emotional resourcefulness. This can help solve problems on the home front.

4 Staying alone today is not a great idea; you may mull over negative feelings. A good run or a workout at the gym will sort it out.

5 Your imagination is working overtime, but your feelings about someone may not be true. Try to see others as they are, not as you would like them to be.

6 You may be excited about sharing an experience with others, only to find that you are giving away too much information. Less is more.

7 You're enjoying someone's companionship, but elements of their personality are irritating you. You have to be subtle in conveying the sorts of changes you would like to see.

8 You'd like someone to partner up or provide support for a business idea, but you feel embarrassed about approaching them. Put your proposal in writing.

9 Don't focus too much on your responsibilities right now or they may overshadow some of the good things that are happening—such as being with the person you love.

10 You'll be frustrated when communicating to bureaucrats, office workers or sales people who don't really care. Quiet assertiveness is a good start.

11 Laziness may have caused you to let someone else handle the detailed aspects of a financial transaction. You need to regain control and take responsibility yourself.

12 If someone doesn't believe in you or your ideas, it means that you haven't convinced them of your commitment. Step it up.

13 Politics could dominate your professional environment, which means that you need to learn the art of war. Look up the ancient Chinese warrior Sun Tzu.

14 Being eccentric pays off today, especially if you've been blending in with the landscape lately. Stand out from the crowd.

15 You may accept some sort of invitation, only to be let down by the outcome. Not every event is going to be stupendous.

16 Just getting out of the house is a great way of blowing off steam today. You need a change of pace along with a change of scenery.

17 You are not prepared for a change of heart from your partner. You need to allow them to express and explore their new-found self.

18 A trip or quiet weekend away with your loved one may seem like a good idea, but only if you have completed all your tasks by their allotted deadlines.

19 Someone's looking up to you at present, but you may not even be aware of it. If you make an error, this could affect their estimation of you.

20 You need to justify your actions to your loved ones, especially if they are a little possessive. Why not share your vision with them to alleviate their fears and insecurities?

21 Someone has a secret, but they don't want to share it, which is very annoying. Is it about you? Don't push too hard as this person will eventually reveal it.

22 Simplify your words as you are likely to get tongue-tied trying to olaborate on the details of a story or instruction. Simplicity is your key word today.

23 Although you want to help someone who is struggling financially, you can see that others are waiting in line. If you help one, you have to help them all.

24 Someone may let you down now, but you may not be aware of the big picture. Consider what you don't know rather than what you do.

25 You're prompted to get your emotions under control and in order. This may be triggered by some self-help program, like Oprah or Dr Phil.

26 You want to do something on the spur of the moment, but the one you want to do it with is a couch potato. You may have to do this independently.

27 As the close of the year approaches, you will be frantically trying to finish everything, especially work that has been obstructed by others. Do what you can.

28 You need to get rid of what you haven't got. Do you know what I mean? The desire for future things is the cause of the problem. Be content with what you have.

29 At the end of a conversation, you'll realise that someone hasn't been paying attention to you. Exit stage right.

30 There has been laxity in some aspect of your financial affairs and you will need to go over your books. Don't be distracted by social events.

DECEMBER

Monthly Overview

The first week of December is excellent, with Venus and Jupiter promising luck, gifts and other positive and satisfying events. Mars entering your zone of social affairs after the 5th highlights your interest in giving back to your peer group and acknowledging their support of you. It will be an excellent close to the year as your ruling planet moves through your zone of career, indicating popularity, additional money, new friends and great expectations for the following year.

1 If you are going to take a shot at someone today, you can do so in a mild and measured manner. It will have the same impact.

2 The problem you have been building up in your mind is not nearly as bad as you think. This will soon become apparent.

3 Try to see the best in your current situation as every cloud has a silver lining.

4 If you listen to gossip, you will come to the same conclusion about an innocent third party. Use discretion to draw your own conclusions.

5 There is good news on the real estate front, particularly if you are looking to re-evaluate the worth of your home. It could be time to consider a move or purchase a second property.

6 If you only have one tool in your tool box, there will be a limit to what you can fix. Likewise, you need variety in your arsenal of personal tools, which means expanding your knowledge base. Psychology is your key word today.

7 A few parties and social engagements will stretch your time to the limit. There is no way out of this and, as you know, Christmas is notorious for this sort of pressure.

8 If those around you are hampering your ability to produce better work, you need to sidestep them to give it your best shot.

9 You're disillusioned by a relationship today, but you've magnified an offhand remark. Don't take things so personally.

10 Working with someone in a temporary environment will bring about a change of pace. Although their style is very different from yours, you can still learn something valuable from them.

11 You need to enhance your actions with supplementary analysis. At present, you're in an industry that is constantly changing. New opportunities will soon arise, so be prepared.

12 There are harmonious planetary alignments at the moment, which means that hard work and fun will go hand in glove. Perfect.

13 You have to wear different hats and do the job of two or three people today. It should be rather busy indeed!

14 Don't confuse friendship with romance. Clearly demarcate which is which, or you are in for trouble.

15 You are lucky at the moment and will receive gifts from people who don't mean that much to you. It just goes to show how little we know!

16 As Christmas approaches, you'll be feeling sentimental, but not in a positive way. Don't allow negative patterns to impinge on what should be a happy, festive period.

17 Overhaul some of your long-term plans, but postpone execution until after Christmas. You have enough on your plate.

18 Complications arise due to the mismanagement of your diary. Pay more attention to timeslots and travel arrangements.

19 You'll find it hard to say no to some pre-Christmas engagements, even though you know that the people present will be as boring as hell. This is the downside of the Christmas period.

20 This year, your traditional Christmas shopping could be more interesting if you go to different stores rather than your usual mall. Today is a day for originality.

21 You can make some breakthrough in your work, which will have a positive impact on your relationships. Spend a little quiet time with the one you love before the Christmas family rush.

22 Making contact with a friend or relative will be a pleasant interlude during the madness of Santa's season. Be careful of excessive phone bills.

23 Make it a point to spend quality time with your parents outside typical social affairs. This could be an excellent bonding opportunity.

24 You've got some great ideas right now, but you need to put them on the backburner with other pressing issues. Last-minute shopping may frazzle you.

25 Merry Christmas, Taurus. The Moon and Sun are at right angles, as are Mercury and Uranus, while the Moon and Mars dominate. This will be a hectic day when you should curtail fiery responses.

26 With the Moon in the eleventh house, this is a much better day for enjoying the company of friends. In-depth discussions are favourable.

27 You'll escape through the back door to sit under a tree and simply do nothing.

28 A new friendship may arise, but don't expect it to be a dazzling, exciting and spontaneous affair. The person may be level-headed rather than excitable.

29 You have a renewed appetite to do extra work, but what's the rush, Taurus? Stop! Enjoy the holiday break for a little longer.

30 Your energy levels should be up, and you're optimistic about what's to come. Family members will make you laugh.

31 It is the final day of the year, and the Moon, Sun and Pluto are all in favourable aspect. You sense a big change coming in the next 12 months!

2014
ASTRONUMEROLOGY

TWENTY YEARS FROM NOW YOU WILL BE
MORE DISAPPOINTED BY THE THINGS
THAT YOU DIDN'T DO THAN BY THE
ONES YOU DID DO. SO THROW OFF THE
BOWLINES. SAIL AWAY FROM THE SAFE
HARBOR. CATCH THE TRADE WINDS IN
YOUR SAILS. EXPLORE. DREAM. DISCOVER.

H. Jackson Brown Jr

THE POWER BEHIND YOUR NAME

Everything in nature is ruled by numbers, including your name and birthday. By simply adding up the numbers of your name, the vibration and ruling planet of this number can be calculated, and through that we can study the effects on your life and destiny. There is an ancient system of numerology that originated in Chaldea. It is somewhat different from the system devised by Pythagoras, but it is equally, if not more, powerful and takes into account the planets and the effects on your name and birthday. Here is a table of the letters, numbers and ruling planets associated with them.

AIJQY	=	1	Sun
BKR	=	2	Moon
CGLS	=	3	Jupiter
DMT	=	4	Uranus
EHNX	=	5	Mercury
UVW	=	6	Venus
OZ	=	7	Neptune
FP	=	8	Saturn
—	=	9	Mars

Note: The number 9 is a spiritual number and, according to the ancient tradition of Chaldean numerology, is not assigned a letter. It is considered an unknowable number. Once the name or birthday numbers have been calculated, the number 9 is used as a sum total number for interpretation.

Throughout history, many people have changed their names for good luck, including actors, writers and musicians. They have done this in the hope of attracting good fortune by using the numbers of the planets connected with that birth date. If you look at the following table of numbers and their meanings, you will have a greater insight into how you can change your name and use this to your own advantage for more fulfilling relationships, wealth, general happiness and success.

Here is an example of how you can calculate the number and power of your name. If your name is Barack Obama, you can calculate the ruling numbers as follows:

B	A	R	A	C	K		O	B	A	M	A
2	1	2	1	3	2		7	2	1	4	1

Now add the numbers like this:

2 + 1 + 2 + 1 + 3 + 2 + 7 + 2 + 1 + 4 + 1   =   26

Then add   2 + 6   =   8

You can now see that the sum total of the numbers is 8, which is ruled by Saturn, and that the underlying vibrations of 2 and 6 are ruled by the Moon and Venus. You can now study the Name Number table to see what these planetary energies and numbers mean for Barack Obama. We can see from Saturn that he is an extremely hard-working and ambitious person with incredible concentration and the ability to sacrifice a lot for his chosen objectives. From Venus and the Moon, we see that he is a person possessing a delightful, charming and persuasive personality, and that he has a strong love for his family.

Name Number	Ruling Planet	Name Characteristics
1	Sun	Being ruled by the Sun means you possess abundant energy and attract others with your powerful aura. You are bright, magnetic and attractive as well. You are generous and loyal in disposition. Because of your high levels of energy, you need sport to make you feel good. You succeed in any enterprise you choose.
2	Moon	You are emotional and your temperament is soft and dreamy, but you must be careful of extreme mood swings. You are psychic and can use your intuitive hunches to understand others and gain an insight into your future. You have strong connections to your mother, family and women in general. Your caring and compassionate nature will make you popular with others.

Name Number	Ruling Planet	Name Characteristics
3	Jupiter	You seem to attract good luck without too much effort, but you must be on guard as you are likely to be excessive even when you are generous. You have strong philosophical instincts and wish to understand why you are here. Travelling is high on your agenda and you will explore many different facets of life and culture. You are a perennial student who wants to learn more about yourself and life in general.
4	Uranus	The number 4 is an unpredictable number, so you need to plan adequately for your life. It will have many unforeseen twists and turns, but you are extraordinarily innovative in the way you deal with life issues. You need unusual friends as you get bored easily, and it's quite likely you will take an interest in technological or scientific things. Learning to be flexible will go a long way in helping you secure a happy and fulfilling life.

Name Number	Ruling Planet	Name Characteristics
5	Mercury	Speed and accuracy are the key words for the planet Mercury and the number 5. You love communication and connect with people easily, but you need to be on guard against dissipating your energies into many frivolous activities. This is a youthful number, and you never grow old. You will always be surrounded by youngsters and people who make you laugh. You have a great sense of humour and will always be successful as you have the gift of the gab.
6	Venus	You have a natural inclination to love and be loved if you are ruled by the number 6 and Venus. Having a delightful personality, you attract many people of the opposite sex. You are successful with money and take great pleasure in working towards your future security. You will have many love affairs, and at some point you may even be torn between two lovers.

Name Number	Ruling Planet	Name Characteristics
7	Neptune	With the number 7 as your ruling number, you have reached a very high level of evolution. You are gifted with premonitions, intuition and clairvoyance. Health and healing are also gifts that you have been endowed with. Learn to discriminate when giving yourself to others.
8	Saturn	You have incredible focus and an ability to achieve anything you set your mind to, no matter how long it takes. You sacrifice for others as your loyalty is highly developed. You work hard to achieve things you believe are worthwhile, but sometimes this overshadows your personal life. You demand that things are done properly, which is why others may not be able to live up to your expectations. Learn to relax a little more.
9	Mars	You have a hot nature and need an outlet such as sport and other physical activities to balance your life and improve your health. You are not afraid of challenges and can be confrontational. Learn to listen and accept that others don't have the same attitudes as you. You are a protector of the family and loyal to the core. You are an individual and never follow another's lead.

YOUR PLANETARY RULER

Numerology is intimately linked to the planets, which is why astrology and your date of birth are also spiritually connected. Once again, here are the planets and their ruling numbers:

1   **Sun**

2   **Moon**

3   **Jupiter**

4   **Uranus**

5   **Mercury**

6   **Venus**

7   **Neptune**

8   **Saturn**

9   **Mars**

Finding your birth numbers is simple. All you have to do is add each of the numbers of your date of birth to arrive at a single digit number. If you're born on 12 November 1972, add the numbers of your day, month and year of birth to find your destiny number, like this:

1 + 2 + 1 + 1 + 1 + 9 + 7 + 2 = 24

Then add   **2 + 4 = 6**

This means that the number 6, which is ruled by Venus, is your destiny number.

YOUR PLANETARY
❧ FORECAST ❧

You can even take your ruling name number and add it to the year in question to throw more light on your coming personal affairs, like this:

B A R A C K O B A M A	=	8
Year coming	=	2014
Add 8 + 2 + 0 + 1 + 4	=	15
Add 1 + 5	=	6

This is the ruling year number using your name number as a basis. Therefore, you would study the influence of Venus (number 6) using the Trends for Your Planetary Ruler in 2014 table. Enjoy!

Trends for Your Planetary Number in 2014

Year Number	Ruling Planet	Results Throughout the Coming Year
1	Sun	

Overview

You are now ready to move forward in a new cycle and create something wonderful for yourself and your loved ones. Your career, finance and personal reputation will improve considerably and your physical health should also be much better. Although there may be some challenges, you're able to meet them head-on and come out a winner.

Love and Pleasure

You can attract anyone you want throughout 2014 because your energy and aura are so strong. You will need many friends and will find yourself doing creative activities alone and with others.

Work

You will have no problem getting a better job or some sort of promotion in your current line of work. More money can be expected, and any changes you make in your life should bring you great satisfaction.

Improving Your Luck

Good luck is on the cards, with July and August being especially lucky for you. The 1st, 8th, 15th and 22nd hours of Sundays are lucky.

Lucky numbers are 1, 10, 19 and 28.

Year Number	Ruling Planet	Results Throughout the Coming Year
2	Moon	

Overview

Although you will feel emotional this year, it's time to take control of yourself and change your personality for the better. Working through issues with females, both at home and in the workplace, may be the key to your happiness and success this year.

Love and Pleasure

Domestic affairs and relationships at home will take centre stage in 2014. Your marital relationship or important significant friendships are high on your agenda of things to improve. You are sensitive and intuitive, so trust your gut feeling when it comes to making decisions in this area of your life.

Work

Make your decisions based on rational thought rather than impulsive emotional reactions. Draw a clear line in the sand between work and leisure for best results. You are more creative this year, so hopefully you will take the opportunity to move along that path rather than doing something you are bored with.

Year Number	Ruling Planet	Results Throughout the Coming Year
2	**Moon**	**Improving Your Luck**

Improving Your Luck

Mondays will be lucky and July will fulfill some of your dreams. The 1st, 8th, 15th and 22nd hours on Mondays are fortunate. Pay special attention to the New and Full Moons in 2014.

Lucky numbers are 2, 11, 20, 29 and 38.

Year Number	Ruling Planet	Results Throughout the Coming Year
3	Jupiter	

Overview

A number 3 year is usually a lucky one due to the beneficial influence of Jupiter. New opportunities, financial good fortune, travels and spiritual insights will be key factors in the coming year.

Love and Pleasure

You have a huge appetite for love, and bond easily with others to fulfil this need. Try to clarify your feelings before investing too much energy into someone who may not be the best choice. This is a year of entertainment and pleasure, and one in which generosity will bring good karma to you.

Work

You can finally ask for that pay rise as this is a lucky year when money will naturally come to you. Promotions, interviews for a new position and general good fortune can be expected.

Improving Your Luck

Don't let harebrained schemes distract you from the practical aspects of life. Good planning is necessary for success. March and December are lucky months. 2014 will bring you some unexpected surprises. The 1st, 8th, 15th and 24th hours of Thursdays are spiritually very lucky for you.

Lucky numbers are 3, 12, 21, and 30.

Year Number	Ruling Planet	Results Throughout the Coming Year
4	Uranus	

Overview

Expect the unexpected with this ruling number for the coming year. If you have spread yourself thinly, then you may lack the requisite energy to handle the changes that are coming. Independence is your key word, but impulse is also likely. Take your time before making important decisions, and structure your life appropriately.

Love and Pleasure

The grass may not be greener on the other side, and if you're feeling trapped in a relationship, you will want to break free of the entanglements that are strangling your self-development. You need to balance tradition with progress if you are to come out of this period a happy person.

Work

Innovation will help you make good progress in your professional life. Learn something new, especially in the technological arena. If you have been reluctant to improve your skill set, you are shooting yourself in the foot. Expand your horizons, learn new tasks and improve your professional future. Group activity will also help you carve a new niche for yourself.

Year Number	Ruling Planet	Results Throughout the Coming Year
4	Uranus	**Improving Your Luck**

Improving Your Luck

Try not to overdo things this year, and learn to be more forbearing with others. Slow and steady wins the race in 2014. Steady investments are lucky. The 1st, 8th, 15th and 20th hours of Saturdays will be very lucky for you.

Lucky numbers are 4, 13, 22 and 31.

| 5 | Mercury | |

Overview

You want to socialise and communicate your feelings this year because you have such a creative and powerful imagination, and it is likely you will connect with many new people. Try not to spread yourself too thinly, as concentration levels may be lacking. Don't be distracted by the wrong crowd.

Love and Pleasure

Reciprocation is important for your relationships in 2014. Variety is the spice of life, but also ensure that your key partnership will weather the storm and get stronger with time. Talk about your feelings, even if this is difficult. Don't be too harsh and critical of the one you love; instead, turn the spotlight of criticism on yourself to improve your character.

Work

People will look up to you in the coming 12 months, which is why new contracts will be drawn and doors will open to provide you with a bright new professional future. You are quick and capable, but try not to overdo things, as this can affect your nervous system. Travel is a great way to balance these energies.

Year Number	Ruling Planet	Results Throughout the Coming Year
5	Mercury	**Improving Your Luck**

Expressing ideas is essential and it will help you come up with great plans that others want to help you with. By being enthusiastic and creative, you will attract the support of those who count. The 1st, 8th, 15th and 20th hours of Wednesdays are your luckiest, so schedule your meetings and other important social engagements at these times.

Lucky numbers are 5, 14, 23 and 32.

Year Number	Ruling Planet	Results Throughout the Coming Year
6	Venus	

Overview

A year of love. Expect romantic and sensual interludes or a new love affair. Number 6 is also related to family life. Working with a loved one or family member is possible, and it will yield good results. Save money, cut costs and share your success.

Love and Pleasure

Love will be important to you, and if you are in a relationship, you can strengthen the bonds with your partner at this time. Making new friends is also on the cards, and these relationships will become equally significant, especially if you are not yet hitched. Engagement, marriage and other important celebrations take place. You will find yourself more socially active.

Work

You have a desire to work on your future financial security, so cutting back costs would be a key factor in this. You may find yourself with more money, but don't let false illusions cause you to spend more than you earn. Developing your part-time interest into a fully-fledged career is also something that can take place this year. Your social life and professional activities will overlap.

Year Number	Ruling Planet	Results Throughout the Coming Year
6	Venus	**Improving Your Luck**

Developing a positive mental attitude will attract good luck and karma that is now ripe for the picking. Enjoy your success, but continue to work on removing those personality defects that are obstructing you from even bigger success. Balance spiritual and financial needs. The 1st, 8th, 15th and 20th hours on Fridays are extremely lucky for you this year, and new opportunities can arise when you least expect them.

Lucky numbers are 6, 15, 24 and 33.

Year Number	Ruling Planet	Results Throughout the Coming Year
7	Neptune	

Overview

You have the power to intuitively understand what needs to be done in 2014. Trust your instincts and make greater efforts at your spiritual and philosophical wellbeing. This is the time when your purpose becomes crystal clear. You can gain a greater understanding of yourself and others and have the ability to heal those who need your help both within and outside your family.

Love and Pleasure

If you can overcome the tendency to find fault with yourself, you will start to truly love yourself and attract those who also love you. This is the key law of success in love, and you will discover this in the coming 12 months. Don't give more than others are prepared to reciprocate. You need to set your standards high enough to meet someone who is worthy of your love.

Work

This is the year to stop watching the clock and produce incredibly wonderful work. No matter how menial the task, you can experience the spiritual significance of work and how this can be used to uplift others. The healing, caring and social services professions may attract you just now.

Year Number	Ruling Planet	Results Throughout the Coming Year
7	Neptune	**Improving Your Luck**

Be clear in your communication so as to avoid misunderstandings with others. If you have some health issues, now is the time to clear them up and improve your general vitality. Sleep well, exercise and develop better eating habits to improve your life. The 1st, 8th, 15th and 20th hours of Wednesdays are your luckiest, so schedule your meetings and other important social engagements at these times.

Lucky numbers are 7, 16, 25 and 34.

Year Number	Ruling Planet	Results Throughout the Coming Year
8	Saturn	

Overview

This is a year of achievement, but it will require discipline and a removal of all distractions to achieve your goals. Eliminating unnecessary aspects of your life that constrict your success will be something you need to pay attention to. Your overall success may be slow, but it is assured.

Love and Pleasure

By overworking, you deny your loved ones the pleasure of your company and emotional support. Take the time to express how you feel. Remember that love is a verb. Spend more time with your loved ones as a countermeasure to excessive work routines.

Work

This is a money year, and the Chinese will tell you that the number 8 is very lucky indeed. But remember that money can't buy you love. Earn well, but also learn to balance your income potential with creative satisfaction.

Year Number	Ruling Planet	Results Throughout the Coming Year
8	Saturn	**Improving Your Luck**

If you are too cautious you may miss wonderful opportunities. Of course, you don't want to make mistakes, but sometimes these mistakes are the best lessons that life can dish out. Have courage and don't be afraid to try something new. The 1st, 8th, 15th and 20th hours of Saturdays are the best times for you in 2014.

Lucky numbers are 1, 8, 17, 26 and 35.

Year Number	Ruling Planet	Results Throughout the Coming Year
9	Mars	

Overview

This is the last cycle, which means that you will be tying up loose ends over the coming 12 months. Don't get caught up in trivial matters as this is the perfect time to redirect your energy into what you want in life. Don't be angry, avoid arguments and clearly focus on what you want now.

Love and Pleasure

You want someone who can return the love, energy and passion that you have for them. If this isn't happening, you may choose to end a relationship and find someone new. Even if you need to transition to a new life, try to do this with grace and diplomacy.

Work

You can be successful this year because of the sheer energy you are capable of investing into your projects. Finish off what is incomplete as there are big things around the corner, and you don't want to leave a mess behind. You can obtain respect and honour from your employers and co-workers.

Year Number	Ruling Planet	Results Throughout the Coming Year
9	Mars	**Improving Your Luck**

Don't waste your valuable energy this year. Use it to discover the many talents that you possess. By doing this you can begin to improve your life in many different ways. Release tension to maintain health. The 1st, 8th, 15th and 20th hours of Tuesdays will be lucky for you throughout 2014.

Lucky numbers are 9, 18, 27 and 36.